Photography by Lindsey Romero

To my daughters,

Murphy and Cooper . . . do you.

No matter what it is.

Please scan the QR code to go to Melissa's website.

www.mascotbooks.com

So You Wanna Be a Hairstylist . . . That's Cute

The author has tried to recreate events, locales, and conversations from their memories of them. In order to maintain their anonymity in some instances, the author has changed the names of individuals and places, and may have changed some identifying characteristics and details such as physical properties, occupations, and places of residence.

Although the author and publisher have made every effort to ensure that the information in this book was correct at press time, the author and publisher do not assume and hereby disclaim any liability to any party for any loss, damage, or disruption caused by errors or omissions, whether such errors or omissions result from negligence, accident, or any other cause.

The views and opinions expressed in this book are solely those of the author. These views and opinions do not necessarily represent those of the publisher or staff.

Cover Photography: Lindsey Romero
Design: Shannon Sullivan

For more information, please contact:
Mascot Books, an imprint of Amplify Publishing Group
620 Herndon Parkway, Suite 220
Herndon, VA 20170
info@mascotbooks.com

Library of Congress Control Number: 2023906032
CPSIA Code: PRV0323A
ISBN-13: 978-1-63755-653-5

Printed in the United States

SO YOU WANNA BE A HAIRSTYLIST

...THAT´S CUTE

MELISSA GOUDEAU

CONTENTS

TAKE A SEAT . . .

I wrote this book mainly for one reason. You'd be shocked at how many clients sit in my chair and tell me their high school student is thinking about not going to college and opting for cosmetology school instead. They rarely say this with enthusiasm. In fact, it's usually with embarrassment or disappointment, which always bothers me. I got super hot and frustrated with one particular client who was already late for her appointment (like always) and sat in my chair so exasperated. She exhaled a deep breath while rolling her eyes and said, "Can you believe my daughter, after all the money I've spent on private schools, wants to go to cosmetology school? What a waste." I stared at her through the mirror's reflection, and I'm pretty sure my eyes burned right through to her brain. Because at that point, she said "Oh, wait. I'm sorry."

I, like so many of my fellow stylists, have had numerous conversations with clients like this. After they've broken the news that their child is choosing cosmetology school, they usually ask, "Do you have any tips for me? Is there anything I can read about this career path?" I usually vomit a bunch of information at this point that probably overwhelms them. After many conversations just like this, I started searching for some sort of book or resource to recommend to them. I came up with zilch—nothing. That's when I decided:

I'm going to write that book myself. Why not? I've worked in three salons, I'm a salon owner myself, I was an English teacher . . . I can do this. I wanted to write a book that will not only give a cosmetologist the upper hand in the industry but also shine a spotlight on a trade skill that the world demands and needs (like so many other trades). I believe that building a successful career in this field of beauty can 100 percent surpass the earnings of a student who went to a university.

This book is for the kids choosing a career in the beauty industry, for the person who wants to change career paths as an adult (like I did), and for the parent who is cheering their child into a kick-ass industry. The world of beauty isn't going anywhere—literally, it will always be here. From Cleopatra to Lady Gaga, behind every great woman was a wildly talented stylist. A person choosing a career in cosmetology has immense opportunities to be as successful as someone who went to college. I'm a firm believer that a college degree isn't for everyone. I wish we'd all stop forcing that down young people's throats. There are creative and skilled people out there in all service industries—cabinetmaking, HVAC, landscaping, roofing, beauty. The best of them are experiencing the same success as college graduates in other fields—sometimes finding more lucrative paths, as their talents are hard to come by.

And I also wrote this book for my two daughters, Murphy and Cooper. One day I won't be here—hopefully, that day is way, way later in life, when they're all grown and being the amazing, accomplished human beings I know they'll be. I want the reassurance that my girls knew with absolute certainty they could be anything they set out to be. I've secretly always made this my mission; I'm not sure if they've noticed yet. If they want to be basket weavers, I want them to be the best damn basket weavers on this entire planet. And if they get tired or bored with weaving baskets, I want them to feel confident that they do not have to stay in that career just because they're comfortable or feel obligated. I want them to dig deeper and envision something else they would like to try. If it's becoming fluent in French while making toilet-bowl scrubbers, then dang it, I hope they tackle that goal—go and be the best French-speaking toilet bowl scrubber–making bosses there ever were. I've been a dancer, cheerleader, student, teacher, choreographer, coach, manager, waitress, bartender, hairstylist, salon owner, and now author. I still have a few things up my sleeve, but I'll leave that for later. So, beautiful daughters, if you're reading this one day, go for it. I don't really care what it is—just do it. And always remember: "You're only as good as the training you do when no one is looking" (my favorite quote).

And I certainly can't forget my husband, David (Davo), who is pretty much the coolest person in my world. After pecking at this book for three to four years—you know, with marriage, two kids, full books behind the chair, and co-owning a twenty-five-person salon, I didn't have much time to write. I finally spilled the beans about it by simply telling him, "Oh, hey, I wrote a book." His facial expression was priceless. I wasn't one bit surprised that he encouraged me, because that's kind of his thing. As a couple, we balance each other perfectly—it's a Libra-Gemini thing.

Then there is my mom, Regina—my role model, my best friend. I thank her for unknowingly helping me in this book-writing endeavor. She instilled in me this drive, for which I give her total credit. No matter what life has thrown her way, she puts on her big-girl panties and deals with it and laughs about it, with a smile on her face. When Dad passed away—I also think he has been motivating me to write this book—my mom pushed on, worked hard, and never let us feel like we weren't a *whole* family. She's broken bones but has come back stronger. When she was diagnosed with cancer, she took the girls swimming and then jumped off the diving board. Nothing stops her. Every day I try my best to emulate my mom, and I hope my girls realize what a hero she is.

Finally, there's my little brother, Clint—my protector, my other half, my confidante, my Buckethead—"You Save Me."

SIDEBAR *WITH* **STEPHANIE KOCIELSKI**

When asked why she wanted to be a hairdresser, Stephanie replied:

"My life was changed by hairstylists. I was 5'7" in kindergarten, and no clothes fit me for my age. My mother's hairstylist made me a Girl Scout uniform and cut my hair so I felt and looked normal. I didn't feel like I was a college kid in first grade anymore. She changed my life.

"Being a hairstylist allows you to go as far as you want to go with your life, surprising yourself as to what other ways your heart can be filled as a human being. When working on clients, we touch their mind, body, and soul—every piece of hair is connected to that client's heart. So it is a gift that we receive daily to work on clients and make them feel their very best."

@kocielski

1 SO YOU WANT TO BE A HAIRSTYLIST?

So you want to be a hairstylist? WTF is wrong with you? Kidding. Well, kind of. In this book, I'm going to be blunt, occasionally harsh, but totally honest. I may even try to talk you out of this. But in the end, I've got your back, and I'm going to try my best to give you the upper hand in this badass world of hair. I'm going to make you feel confident about your next move—maybe even a little cocky about it. I'd love you to write all over the pages of this book—make a mess, highlight it all up. It's yours anyway. Who cares? We're not only going to get you successfully through school, but together we're going to help you be the top dog that salons are fighting for when you finish.

Why are we hairstylists important? Let me tell you. Since ancient times, cosmetology was derived from servants making the people they worked for beautiful. Being pampered and fanned while others took care of their skin, nails, and hair was a sign of wealth. Throughout history, cosmetologists, even though they weren't named that yet, set the tone for the looks of that time period. It was us. We brought the pin curls, the Farrah Faucet hair, the shag bangs, the Beetles bangs, the Twiggy eyeliner, the skateboarder cuts, the fresh fades with lightning bolts, the *Golden Girl* perms—that was us. The evolution of our field started long ago and has transformed with every passing decade and century. So yeah, those other professions are supercool and all, but we're the cool ones who leave the trends behind.

But before I go on, a word for the readers who are in this for the "cute" crap: If you're going to cosmetology school because you like the glitter, the smoky eye, and you've done a few updos on some friends for high school dances, you better dig a little deeper than that, honey. There are lots of girls and guys who have a knack for that. Do you know how many people out there do other people's hair in high school? Do other friends' makeup for a party? That's cool you can do that and all, but that doesn't mean you should be a stylist.

Think about it: almost everyone on the planet has hair. Most women—and some men—wear makeup at some point in their life, if not every day. What makes you special? What's going to separate you from them? Why didn't they just become stylists and makeup artists? What makes you think they're going to spend their hard-earned money on something they could probably do themselves?

Just having a cute love for hair and makeup and watching a few YouTube and TikTok videos on how-tos will not make you a great stylist. You need a lot more than that. You'll need *hunger* and *hustle*. Those two words are the most discussed attributes between my business partner and me in all our after-interview conversations. We receive résumés all the time, but the first thing we do is look at their social media for their work. Is it legit? Does it look like they have potential? Then we look at their social media to make sure they're not batshit crazy in their personal life (drunken party photos, bashing other individuals, things of that nature). We gather as much info on them as we can from people who know them, went to school with them, worked with them, or have friends or family in common with them. We have a good relationship with the cosmo schools in our area and sometimes call to ask about a particular student (though we rarely hire people right out of school). Last, we do all we can to find out if they have *hunger* and *hustle*. I could not be more serious about this. Sometimes we'll hire a newer stylist who we can tell wants to learn so badly over a veteran stylist who may have an "OK" clientele, but who is so stuck in their old ways that they don't want to learn new things. But then again, not all new stylists are hungry. Sometimes you can tell when they don't have much drive. And more importantly, not all veterans are cocky and stubborn. For example, our experienced stylists in our salon are always traveling to hair shows, signing up for online classes, killing the game. But honestly, as owners, if you're trying to come and work at our salon, young or old, we're looking for hunger and hustle—period.

If you take a look at the most successful stylists on social media, I guarantee they've had some insane hustle and hunger to get where they are right now. If you're going to do this, do it right. Don't half-ass it. If you're thinking you're just going to walk into hair school and walk out and start making a six-figure income, you're wasting your money and time. If you want to make a career out of this—and I'm talking about the type of career where you can stand on your own and pay your own bills and buy your own house and car—start treating this career with some respect. Do your homework now; set yourself up to be a sought-after stylist. Let me help you.

The misconception: You're going to get out of hair school and have a clientele because you have some family and friends to start up on, and you think a few of the people from school will follow you. Negative, my friend. Unless you come from a lot of money and don't *need* to work, those first few years out of hair school are brutal. I had to wait tables while in hair school and for about a year or so after hair school too. This little paragraph is super important. You will not get out of school and have full books. In fact, you'll most likely not have any appointments at all. I need you to start getting a plan together, or at least forming an idea for some backup money as you go through school and those first few years. Trust me, you'll feel better about this and so will your parents or guardians in you picking this as a career. The money you'll be losing in that first year by not being booked and buying the supplies and products you need kind of sucks. If you create that backup plan now—waiting tables or some sort of side hustle—those first years won't be so crappy, and you won't feel so broke. I'm going to break down all this aggravating money stuff a little later on. You'd be surprised at how many people give up on styling during their first year because they can't survive financially. Out of the fourteen people who

Me and my cute business partner, sister-in-law, and partner in crime—Catherine Goudeau Brignac.

started my month in cos school, I only know of one other person who made it in this field. That makes me sad.

Before we move on, let me do a little quick sum-up of myself . . . .

I grew up with super crappy hair, in a time when flat irons were not invented yet, in Natchez, Mississippi. I had to learn how to fix my curly, nasty, frizzy, awkward hair because no one else could. Fast-forward to Lafayette, Louisiana, where we moved when I was in elementary school. Still, no stylist could do my hair. After visiting a salon, I would go home and cry and fix it myself. I ended up being a pretty smart kid in high school, receiving some scholarships for academics and dancing, and was being sent to college with a lot of money. But I didn't want to go to college. I wanted to be a hairstylist. My mom (public school teacher of thirty-six years) thought I was crazy for not going to college, and I would be throwing money in the trash if I didn't take this free money they were giving me to get a degree. So I went to college, got a degree in English, went and taught honors English at a local high school, and was the cheerleading sponsor. I actually liked teaching; it just wasn't doing it for me. I *still* wanted to do hair.

I called my then fiancé and asked if I could quit teaching and go to cosmetology school. He thought I was crazy, but he trusted me. So I did it at twenty-nine years old. I'm now at my third salon, and I happen to own it with my beautiful sister-in-law, Catherine Goudeau Brignac, who is a very talented stylist. It's a huge salon with twenty stylists—some of the best in Lafayette, Louisiana. We've won multiple awards for best salon, and we're also the top-selling Paul Mitchell Focus salon in Louisiana. I'm also certified in a few other things, like keratin treatments, and I'm a master in Invisible Bead Extensions.

Now that you know I was a teacher (among many other jobs), I'd like to state that I do not regret my pathway to this career. You shouldn't either. Maybe you're a bartender thinking about doing this later on—do it. That high multitasking skill and ability to handle so many types of personalities will benefit you as a stylist. Maybe you're working in a tanning salon and want to be a stylist. You already know how to work a booking system and explain products and how to sanitize the stations properly—all things a stylist does. Maybe you were on a team (cheer, track, whatever), so you already know how to work with others and practice your hardest to obtain a particular goal—same as a stylist. No career path is linear. This is an inescapable truth, and it's something young people (even matured adults stuck in another field) don't often hear. Don't think that some part of your job, however new or experienced you are in it, won't help you in cosmetology. And it's never too late to change careers, I did it at twenty-nine, and I would do it again at forty-two if I knew it would make me happy.

OK, that's me. As a successful stylist and business owner, I feel there has been a gap or hole left from when a person decides to get into cosmetology until they become a financially stable stylist. Though cosmetology school teaches you the skills to pass your state board exam, no one ever explains to a newbie the real "behind the scenes" nitty-gritty part of the field. That's what I'm here to do. Now that you know what we look for when hiring and the myths of newly graduated stylists just going out there and crushing this career, I'm going to break down each facet of this beauty world for you to help you navigate your path and prepare yourself so that your entry into this profession runs smoothly with few speed bumps. We'll learn about the money, the tools, the good and the crap parts, how to be top of your class, and how to land your dream salon. Buckle up, friend, you're doing this.

2 BY NOW . . .

This chapter is about how to have that conversation with your parents or guardians—or just yourself, if you're trying to switch careers like I did. I'm giving you some tips on having that "conversation" about choosing to go into cosmetology and not a four-year college.

Right about now, you probably have the jitters. That's cool; that's normal. You might be afraid others will think you're crazy. That's cool, too, because you probably are—own it. Society drills it into our brains that college is the answer, and for a lot of people that is completely true. But all those college graduates will become managers, doctors, lawyers, etc., and who do you think they'll pay the good money to look the part? You—that is, if you brand yourself and feed your talent and stay on top of your game. When I asked Mark Palermo, the (newly retired) CEO of Vanguard Paul Mitchell Systems, what he thought the scariest part of cosmetology school was, he said, "Fear of the unknown is a natural emotion. Starting something big can be very exciting . . . and a little scary. This can be a good thing so long as you get the 'butterflies' to fly in formation. You can do this by immersing yourself in your cosmo program—be all in. Do so and you'll have those butterflies flying in formation in no time." Organize yourself, push through, and everything will fall into place.

You're probably thinking others may think of you as an educational failure since you didn't choose college—prove them wrong. You're probably thinking your parents or guardians will fight you on this because they've always dreamed you'd get a degree. They might. That's OK. To get them off your back, tell them it's just for a year and a half, and if you don't like it, you can go to college—but we both know you're gonna kill this. If you read this book and complete the tasks we've discussed, you are 100 percent setting yourself up for success. If you treat this career with intent, you're training yourself from the beginning to build your own brand and have your bank account reflect it. Shake those jitters out, face those parents or others—or yourself, for that matter, if you just need to make this decision for yourself because you're unhappy in your current career. So many times I find myself wishing I would've gone straight to hair school instead of college. But then I wouldn't be here writing this book with confidence from my English degree. We all have different paths, and that's cool. We take these paths for a reason. You may not see that reason now, but you will—I'm pretty confident about that.

By now, you've had to at least found that fire in yourself. You've most likely watched a crapload of videos on how to style, perform updos, do makeup, and possibly do a color service. That's cool. You'll *never* stop doing this. *Ever.* This is the best way to learn—I swear by it. When you're about to sleep, when you're in the waiting room, watch a video. Soak it in. Never become that old stylist who won't learn new tricks, who are so stuck in their ways that they slowly start losing clients to stylists who are better than them. Never get so cocky that you don't think you can learn from others. Trust me—I've seen a newer stylist who's only been at a salon for a year or two whose books are getting full because they stay up-to-date on trends and are always perfecting their skills—and then I've seen a veteran stylist who finished school like ten years ago who only has a handful of clientele and is always waiting on walk-ins.

PRO TIP

Practice on your friends and family as much as possible. Practice blow-drying, watch braid videos and use them as models, and try some DIY tricks you learned on them. Muscle memory in your hands is a real thing. Get ahead of the game.

Don't be that type of veteran stylist. Keep up. Stay relevant, don't get cocky, and never stop educating yourself. By now, you've realized you have a fire. Feed it; don't lose it. Don't be that veteran stylist I was just talking about who just shows up to work and never improves. Keep that fire lit, my friend.

And by now, you've had the "discussion" with your parents or guardians, or you're getting pretty close to having it. Or maybe you've bought this book because *you* are just trying to decide for yourself. Surprisingly, this conversation

This is Cami Ezernack, the stylist I mention in the acknowledgments. She always stays ahead of the game; she's always following amazing artists and takes extra classes on the side to keep ahead of everyone else.

is super hard for some people. Even if it's just you who gets to make this decision, and you're trying to feel comfortable in telling your friends who might think you're insane for choosing this field. Read this chapter—preferably this entire book, if you believe they'll be hard to persuade—and start gathering all your ammo for the big convo.

There's a huge misconception that students who choose a trade school, like cosmetology, are not smart enough to go to a university. Yeah, I laugh at that. I was a massive nerd, with great grades and honors classes and a leader in every club or team they'd let me participate in. I know plenty of stylists with college degrees—one of ours is a biology major. That degree is a phenomenal accomplishment; I have one myself. But numerous stylists can easily make the same income, if not greater, as those with even a master's degree. So that myth of a college degree being better than a stylist license is kind of bullshit. Again, you dictate what your bank account looks like. That statement is true in most career fields. So when someone tries to direct you away from this field by saying you won't make enough money, call their bluff. Highlight parts of this book to prove your point and regurgitate it to them.

Do you know how scared I was telling everyone I was leaving my stable teaching job to go to hair school? What would they think of me—a dreamer, an idiot, insane? I was embarrassed and thought they'd make fun of me for chasing a "little girl's dream." I felt my family would think I had lost my mind because I did so well in college to get my English degree, and now I was giving that all up to go curl some hair. I just knew my friends would think I was an idiot for giving up my health insurance, benefits, salary, and retirement to go wait tables while I was in hair school. But I had a fire in me for hair since middle school, and if I didn't let it out, I'd feel trapped. I didn't like my monotonous job, even though I knew I was pretty good at it. I was deathly afraid of telling my principal about my new endeavor. I knew I was a strong teacher in his eyes, so I just knew he'd be pissed at me. But one day while on lunch duty at school, he came up to me.

"So, Pittman, I hear you're wanting to go to hair school." My face turned beet red, and I knew I had pit sweat.

"Yes sir, it's something I've always wanted to do."

He surprised me with, "Well, then you need to go. You're one of my best teachers, but I want you to go make yourself happy before you get stuck in this field and feel trapped. Go before you get too far in and feel like you have to complete it for retirement."

To this day, I can't believe he said that, and I'm so thankful he did. That was the boost of confidence I needed to start pursuing this dream head-on. So, Mr. Craig, if you're ever reading this book, thank you.

TALKING POINTS FOR THE "BIG CONVO"

1. College degrees aren't for everyone.
    - One antiquated stigma is that everyone should go to college. Find a major, go to a four-year college and get a degree, blah blah blah. That's great and all, but in my opinion, sometimes college is overrated. Think about it: How many people do you know *actually* work in the field they have a degree in, besides health-care workers and lawyers? I even know teachers without a teaching degree. I've had friends who started out at the very bottom of a company and now they're some of the top dudes—and they never went to college! I have friends and family who make a killing by doing technical jobs and opening up their own small businesses and never even went to college—AC company, cabinetmakers, pool-installation companies, roofing companies. There are hairstylists who can easily make a six-figure income—shoot, celebrity hairstylists make millions. A four-year college degree isn't the answer for everyone; I can't preach that enough. You don't always have to follow the majority.
        - In your convo, give examples of successful friends and family members who didn't go to college.
        - Ask them how much they've paid trade people to fix their AC, to put on a new roof, to fix their engine.

Ask them how much they've paid over the years to fix their hair.

2. Find out some top stylists' salaries in your area.
    - If you can be snoopy and develop a good relationship with your hairstylist, ask them some financial roundabouts for a *good* stylist in your area. Ask that stylist what some of their top stylists make—and tell them it's so you can talk your parentals into going into hair school.
        - In your convo with your parentals, discuss this gathered info of what the top stylists in your area are making.

3. Show them the stats of good cosmo schools in your area.
    - Look prepared. Go ahead and read a few more of the chapters in this book—about searching for schools and starting your toolbox. Then, when you go into your convo, show them this book you've already bought, the toolbox you've already started, and the research you've done on the local schools. All of this will show you're getting serious about it.

4. Show them all the different facets of this industry.
    - Mention all the side avenues you can take in this field—lash artists, makeup artists, extensions specialists, etc.
    - Show them that you have so many choices in this world of beauty.

5. You've made financial plans for this decision.
    - Make sure you've already gotten a side job in mind.
    - Later I'll tell you about student loans that are occasionally available.
    - Commission salons can also help take away the burden of starting in this field.

6. If they're hesitant about it, remind them:
   - You can get financial assistance, and you don't have to start paying it until after you graduate hair school;
   - It's only for about a year, so if you finish and you don't like it, you haven't wasted that much time;
   - You'll be able to get a job while you're in school, and you'll do their hair for free (ha-ha); and
   - Anything else you think will let you get into this demanding industry.

So you found the fire in you. It's a legit craving to explore this artistic world that makes others beautiful by your own hand. Schools are so important. We once hired a girl simply because she went to a Paul Mitchell School. So go find a school—extra points if you do this *before* you talk to your parentals; it'll make the "adulting" experience a little more authentic.

Next, you need to find the right school for you. Here's how to go about it.

HOW TO RESEARCH THE SCHOOLS IN YOUR AREA

1. Find out if the school is Monday–Friday or Tuesday–Saturday, which will be your schedule for the rest of your life. See which schedule and times work the best for you.

2. Tour every school! If you call and say you want to tour, the schools love that. That's literally what they're supposed to do, so don't feel stupid. Bring a friend, parent, or go by yourself. But go to all of them.

3. The next part is tricky—you'll have to do some investigative work. Figure out what the statistics are on how many people actually pass their boards from each school. You can ask around, you can call the school directly. In Lafayette, for example, there are four cosmetology schools. I know which one produces the best outcome at boards. This is just through conversation and realizing this over the years by

working with all types of stylists in our area. When you get your hair done next, just ask your stylist which school has the best passing rate and what they thought about their school. Ask them where most of their stylists went to school.

4. Find out how many months it takes to graduate at that particular school. For instance, Louisiana asks for a certain number of hours in the classroom and on the salon floor during cosmetology school. Some schools just rearrange those hours differently. Some schools in Lafayette are arranged to take you fifteen months to finish cosmetology school. One of those schools only takes twelve months—you'll just have longer days at school within that year. See which setup you like. You can look up your state's guidelines and hours to better prepare yourself.

5. See how much each one costs and if they have payment plans, scholarships, grants, etc. Some will help you sign up for a student loan. You may have to go and get your first loan at a bank, and you'll probably need a cosigner, unless you're bad and bougie. Most of these loans you won't have to pay back until you graduate.

6. Last, let's be honest, you'll more than likely have to have a job while you're in hair school. So keep this in mind when you're picking the school you want to go to—make sure it's close to work and works with your schedule. You may even need to keep this job when you start in a salon, until you build up a strong clientele.

Look official and get yourself a notebook, binder, or journal and fill out this information for each school. It will make you feel so nerdy, yet so prepared.

Pick your school. Do the dirty work and get signed up. While you're waiting to enroll, don't just sit there—get on social media and start searching for inspiration. Find awesome tools, products, and how-tos!

School Name: ______________________________

Address: ______________________________

How long to graduate: ______________________________

How much: ______________________________

School provide loan? ______________________________

Passing rate at boards: ______________________________

Week Schedule? ________________________

School times? ______________________________

What are the uniforms you have to wear? ______________

____

What comes in your starter kit? __________________

____

____

____

____

____

____

____

3 SO CAN YOU MAKE BANK IN THIS?

I don't know. Can you? I need you to seriously *hear* me when I say this: If you become a stylist, *you* will dictate how much money you will make. Your work ethic will dictate your earnings. I mean this so much. If you are just chill and wait for clients to come to you and just do an OK job on every person who sits in your chair, you will in turn make OK money, if that. If you'd like to stand on your own two feet and buy everything yourself, with no help, you legit can do it. I mean this with every fiber of my being.

Cosmetology has become one of the most profitable businesses in the world. And it all depends on how well you set yourself apart from others. It's about your hustle, your hunger, and your brand.

Let's talk about the word *brand*. I'm not talking about the brand of products you use. I'm talking about branding yourself. Start dressing your part and setting yourself apart from the others. Maybe your dress is hippie or funky or eccentric or trendy or punk. Start owning your look and being yourself. Your brand usually attracts the type of client you want. This doesn't mean you're excluding an entire demographic; it just means you're making yourself your own person. Branding can also mean the way you handle your business. Are you relaxed and aloof about your scheduling? "Sure, I can take you next

Thursday. If I have someone then, I'll just juggle both of you. We'll just figure it out." Or maybe you're super efficient and have your scheduling and pricing so well thought out that your business functions like a well-oiled machine. Maybe you're known as a neat freak—the best—and keep your station orderly and sanitize every surface and tool immaculately. Maybe your social media is hilarious and shows you keep a fun environment at your chair. Maybe your social media shows you're trendy, and you're obsessed with education and like to try new things. Maybe your brand is updos and makeup, and that's what you choose to focus on. Branding is just setting yourself apart from others, giving yourself a reputation that you're proud of. Get it? Now go brand yourself.

Maddie Grabert made a name for herself before she even got to cosmetology school. She started doing makeup on her friends in high school. Those friends told friends from other high schools. By the time she finished school and assisted with me for one month, her books were already full. If you see her social media page, her brand has already been set, and people know what they're getting with her.

Work on your look (your brand). When you go to places, make people ask, "Who did your makeup and hair?" At our salon, we like to dress up every day—outfit, makeup, and hair. It's trendy now to have a relaxed look, and we encourage that (if done correctly—no yoga pants like you just left the gym). But you still need to have your hair and makeup like you really care about your job. Train yourself now into creating an image for yourself. We always say, "If a client comes in and all the stylists make a line, and the client has to pick which stylist they want, make them pick you." Most clients will pick the female stylist whose hair, makeup, and attire is on point, or the male stylist who exudes a cool, but professional, vibe.

Picture this: You get your first stylist job—let's pretend it's just a simple, small salon. You show up every day dressed to kill, even if the others are in sweatshirts and tennis shoes. You don't care; you level up. I mean, your hair and makeup are on point—no matter how you're feeling that day or how little sleep you got that night. Others may say you're extra. That's OK. Be extra. Like, if a photographer came in randomly any day to get a few shots for a local magazine, you are so ready. You don't slip on this dress-up aspect. Even when you're feeling bad or sad, you still dress like a beast. I don't care if you got in a fender bender, your fish died, and you have six big zits on your forehead. You walk in that salon looking like a whole celebrity every day. I don't care if it's a mom-and-pop salon with two chairs, a chain salon, or a huge salon. You dress the way you want your bank account to look. Next, each walk-in or friend—let's be honest, those are your first clients anyway—who sits in your chair gets treated like a famous person. You take your time, you teach them how to fix and style their hair daily on their own, and you sell them products because now they *believe* they must have *everything* you used because they've never looked so fabulous. And guess what happens next—they tell a friend, they tell a coworker, they tell a relative. I promise you this: if this does not happen to you, then you did not do what I explained above, plain and simple. If you take one paragraph from this entire book to live by, choose this paragraph. Dress to your brand and give each client the best treatment they've ever experienced sitting in a stylist's chair. Watch your appointment book fill up.

If you do everything in the previous paragraph, your clientele will grow, and with that, you'll *outgrow* your salon. Keep your eyes on the prized salon you'd like to work at next. Make the move; don't settle. If you do this, and sometimes repeat to move to an even better salon, I guarantee your bank account will reflect the effort.

And about moving to another salon: Keep in mind that brand I was talking about. You can figure out if you'd like to be in a bougie salon, an edgy salon, a rocker salon, a hippy-looking salon, a girly salon—the possibilities are endless. Figure out the brand (your look) and then find a salon that matches that spirit, where you'll feel at home. On the other hand, maybe your goal is to have longevity at a salon and stay there forever. We've had bomb-ass stylists who have been with us since we opened nine years ago, and their reputations far precede them. Everyone knows exactly where to find them—the Cut House Salon. When you stay somewhere a long time, you're making your reputation known around town. So whether you're already at an amazing salon or you're working yourself through the ranks to be at a better salon, start branding yourself, and you'll reach your money goal.

> Your own personal brand distinguishes you from others: it's what makes you different or unique. Whether you think about it or not, you are a brand, and if you are confused about your brand, *your customers will be confused, too.*
> *—Business Fundamentals: Connecting to My Future*

Maybe you have a fashion-forward style, and your social media work reflects that. Whatever your brand is, embrace it.

For the people who *don't* make money in this field, it's usually because they have a poor work ethic, no brand, and are lacking hunger and hustle. I've seen stylists who have been doing hair for years live financially month to month and mainly wait on walk-ins and do an OK job with everyone. They will blame their lack of clients and money on everything but themselves—they'll blame the salon, the community, their homelife, their stress, their lack of sleep, you name it. If you have been in this industry for a long time, and you still have open spots on your books every week, you need to step back and be honest with yourself. Ask yourself these questions: Is it my work? Does my clientele feel like I don't care? Does my appearance look like I don't care? Is my work mediocre? Am I stuck in my old ways? Am I charging too much for the experience and result I'm giving them? If you answered yes to any of those questions, *you* are the problem. *Period.* You are the reason your bank account looks like it does. Sorry if this sounds harsh, but I told you that I'd be honest. Zippia.com did a study on almost twenty-five thousand cosmetologists and less than 20 percent of those stylists stayed in the field for more than eleven years.* That number is disheartening but proves the point of brand, hunger, and hustle that we talked about. Had the 80 percent of stylists in that survey who didn't last ten years in the industry worked hard at establishing their brand, hunger, and hustle, they would have realized how lucrative this field is.

I've also seen stylists move here from other towns and not know a soul, and in one year or two have booked-up schedules and buy themselves their own house or car with no help. I've seen single-mom stylists go through a divorce and get hardly anything from it and work their asses off and within a year buy their own homes and cars. It's a beautiful thing. With this career, you get out of it what you put in. It's just that simple. It's all about communicating your brand and having that hunger and hustle—that is how you make money in this industry.

Like I said, money will be tight in the beginning. While I was in school, and about one to two years after graduation and working in a salon, I worked as a waitress to make up for my "not full" books. I was building a clientele, and I had some days without one client booked. That's how everyone starts—empty books; expect it. Don't be naive; be prepared. But after using all the steps mentioned above—hunger, hustle, brand—money wasn't an issue anymore. You *can* make bank in this.

You decide how much money you'll make in this career. If you just want to be a chill stylist—I'm not saying that negatively; for some people, that's actually

* "Hair Stylists, Demographics and Statistics in the US." (Zippia, September 9, 2022) http://zippia.com/hair-stylists-jobs/demographics/.

You'll notice my business partner, Catherine Goudeau Brignac, is cute as a button. She could have literally had the worst day of her life, and she legit comes to work every single day as if she were shooting the cover of a magazine.

a goal—and have pretty calm workdays or not work much and not put much into your own education, your bank account will reflect that. And if you're cool with that, then do you, baby.

If you hustle and turn out good work and spend those extra minutes explaining to your client how to fix their hair at home, your books *will* fill. If you spend like an hour a week or even a month learning something new in this field and applying it to your clients, your books will fill. These people will refer other people. You won't even need to advertise, though I highly recommend that you do. If you do all these things, *your books will fill*, and your bank account will reflect this. I promise you this.

My proudest moments as a salon owner are when one of our stylists buys their first house on their own or their first car without anyone cosigning for it. I genuinely get giddy inside. I feel like a proud mama; as I type this, my hair is standing up on my arms. It's like seeing a light bulb go off in their head. They worked their asses off, they worked the late nights, they sat there on slow days waiting for walk-ins—who are still loyal to only them to this day—and they all did the damn thing.

There are stylists in my hometown who make $30,000 a year and stylists who make over $100,000 a year. The best way to explain that in "cost of living" terms for our town of Lafayette, Louisiana, is a fifteen-hundred-square-foot home can cost between $150,000 and $300,000 depending on the area of town, and an average women's haircut costs about $30 to $35 dollars at most salons (more experienced stylists are more at the $45 to $55 level). The national average pay for hairstylists, according to the Bureau of Labor Statistics, is an hourly wage of $14.41.* This number will vary not only by the area you live in but also by the type of salon you work in and your experience. Some stylists in our area can average $100 to $125 an hour, but this number can be misleading in that some of that money goes to supplies, products, booth rent, and other costs of being a stylist.

* "Barbers, Hairstylists, and Cosmetologists." (US Bureau of Labor Statistics, September 13, 2002) http:// bls.gov/ooh/personal-care-and-service/ Barbers-hairstylists-and-cosmetologists.htm.

This is our stylist, Jordan Prioux Toups. She's one of the hardest-working stylists I know. She's one of those stylists who can juggle two to three clients at a time, unlike me. She comes in early and is closing the salon down most of the time. She's a hustler, for sure.

According to the Bureau of Labor Statistics, there will be approximately 64,400 more cosmetologists, hairstylists, and barbers in the year 2024 than there were in 2014.* This 10 percent growth rate is pretty good, considering the national average for all careers combined is closer to 7 percent (Bureau of Labor Statistics). Cosmetology isn't going anywhere, no matter how many "how-to" videos go viral. Treat your job with such professionalism and respect, even if others in your salon don't, and watch yourself rise above and pass them all.

Even in tough times, people want their hair done. Louisiana is big in the oil industry. I've seen times when the oil industry was in a pretty rough state, and around here everyone is related to *someone* in the oil industry. I had clients whose husbands lost their jobs, but let me tell you, they didn't want their gray roots to show they were going through hard times. They still budgeted for their hair. Side note: I always try to help my clients who are having financial problems by suggesting they skip a haircut or some other services, without revealing that I know they are going through hard times. I didn't want to embarrass them. My point is, there will always be a need for the beauty industry. The Avenue Five Institute states that "hair coloring services jumped 2.6 percent thanks to the Baby Boomers looking to cover up their gray hair."† No matter what people are going through in their personal and financial life, some just do not like for their gray hair to show.

PRO TIP

When you're starting out, you can hand out business cards with discounts, or you can volunteer yourself to do hair and makeup for all the photographers in your area. If that photographer posts their work and mentions you, that's the best advertisement besides client referrals.

Mark Palermo, CEO of Vanguard Paul Mitchell Salon Systems, described the American dream as

* "Barbers, Hairstylists, and Cosmetologists."

† Avenuefive.edu. 2022 Avenue Five Institute. "Important Cosmetology Industry Statistics."

follows: "The promise for potential success and prosperity, the belief that anyone, regardless of where they were born or which class they were born into, can attain their own version of success and prosperity in a society where upward mobility is possible for everyone." I felt that quote deeply. You can blame your upbringing for so long, until it handicaps you. Your future depends on you and only you. You can be so successful in this field—and any field, for that matter—if you only have the hunger and hustle to be your best, no matter

This pic is one of our former receptionists, Ali Fontenot. She was in a small town in a two-chair salon and worked on her off days at our front desk. She recently started as a stylist with us, and although she's starting with brand-new empty books in a new town, she stays all day, waiting for walk-ins. But once she's done someone's hair, they almost always rebook with her. Her books are growing rapidly, and we couldn't be prouder.

your past. Mark also stated, "Your personal potential and possibility will correlate directly with two distinct traits: (1) your talents within your craft (your aptitude) and (2) a burning desire to achieve success (your attitude)."*

Yes, if you have hunger, hustle, a brand, and a never-ending thirst for education you will thrive. Like most professions, however, you may have lulls in your day, week, month, or year. You will have competition with other rising stars in your area whose reputation is surpassing yours at moments in your career. Maybe a new hot salon is opening in your area. Maybe another salon's stylist is taking off on social media, and everyone wants to try them out. All of this will happen; expect it. Clients are always looking for the new, hot, trendy stylist just like they're chasing the new, hot, trendy fashion. We have stylists leave for other salons seeing if the grass is greener, and that is ok. It took me a while to figure that out, but it is sincerely ok. Some stylists think "the grass is always greener" at another salon. With time and experience comes wisdom and you realize the end of that popular quote—"the grass is always greener where you water it." All new stylists and new salons popping up go through their "honeymoon" phases where everything is new and shiny and everyone is talking about them. That's OK—let them have their spotlight and time to shine. But if you stay in your spot, kill it with your hunger, hustle, brand, education, and social media, their spotlight will fade. Better yet, if you're rock solid in those aspects, your clients will never budge. They know they've got a diamond, and no one knows their hair like you do. Show patience and humility and actually cheer those other stylists and salons on; there's enough hair in your town for everyone. Never trash talk another stylist or salon; it will always come back to bite you. Plus, it shows they're not your competition; you are your competition. Cheer them on and wish them luck.

To sum it up, you can make money in this career choice. You literally determine how much money you make. I can't stress this entire chapter enough.

---

* Brennan Claybaugh et al. *Business Fundamentals: Connecting to My Future.* (Louisiana: Vanguard Publishing, 2018) ix.

SIDEBAR *WITH* **LARISA LOVE**

To really set yourself up for future success and set yourself up financially in the future, listen to what Larisa Love says about the beginning of your career:

"My top advice for beginners is to find a mentor—someone who will invest their time into you and show you their ways and really show you how to be the best stylist you can be. If it turns out the first one you go to is not it, it is OK to move around until you find someone who truly cares for your future and your career."

@Larisadoll

4 THE CRAP PART

Like any career, cosmetology does have its crap. It's not all glamorous. Remember: I told you that I'd be honest. I'll live up to my word. Please don't let this chapter scare you too much. I just want to make sure you go in prepared and don't have any unexpected turns that might interrupt your schooling or your dream of being a top-notch stylist.

1. You are on your feet all day—at least if you're doing hair. Find your kicks. Example, if I wear flats, I hurt at the end of the day. But if I wear wedges, I'm actually OK. I only wear heels on short days. We have all genders at our salon, and with a little tweaking to our contract it's cool if they wear tennis shoes, as long as their outfit is bomb—they never disappoint.
    - Perk to this—when I was preggo, I pretty much ate anything because I was on my feet all day, and I worked it off. You will get your steps in, so it actually keeps you in shape.
    - And if you really pay attention to that chapter in cos school, they teach you how to hold your arms and back. This is important. *You have to stretch every day.* I get made fun of at work a lot because I'm constantly stretching; however, it's

kind of funny because now I see some of them doing the same (because it helps!).

2. It's likely that when you get to a full-book point in your career, you'll either be a workhorse, or you'll be smart and block off your days and times that suit you. My point is, the hours can be brutal.
   - I've finally gotten to a point in my career where I've blocked off every other Saturday. It took me over a decade to get to this point, but my family and I deserve this. I'm booked out solid for about three to four months, and I leave early on Fridays and Saturdays.
   - Another good point is, as you become a veteran, you can start designing your calendar and services you'd like to offer. For instance, I stopped taking "just haircuts." I still cut my color and extension clients but stopped taking services that were just a haircut (women's, men's, kid's, dry, etc.). Most stylists love cutting, and I do too. I just came to a point in my career where I needed to choose what my favorites were while catering to my ideal schedule.

3. You'll have to learn strict sanitation, disinfection, and sterilization requirements if you'd like to be respected. Would you want a hairbrush in your hair that has been used in hundreds of heads and never disinfected? Some stylists are gross—don't be them. It takes extra time, but do it.

4. A lot of people fail one part of their cosmetology test. It's cool. It sucks, but it's cool. Study what you need to and go do it again. A lot of us are in this industry because we're *not* big school people or test-takers. Don't be so hard on yourself. Plus, no one has ever asked me if I passed my test on the first try, and I've never asked anyone else either.

This is Lainey Eastin applying root color to a client. Do you know how long it takes a stylist to become comfortable formulating colors to change a client's natural color and existing color and to all be cohesive? Years—it takes years. And even then we still ask for help to make sure.

If you look closely at my fingers in this pic, they're disgusting. There's literally color all over my fingers, and I'm sporting a Band-Aid. This will be your life.

5. There is mathematics and chemistry involved in this. It will be scary at first, but after a while it gets so ingrained in your brain that you just spit that crap out like you're speaking another language, and it looks super impressive to others. For example: "I believe I'll start with a 4N and a dab of 3A with 20 cream equal parts and root that all over while pulling longer in the back for a halo effect. I'll use lightener and 20 cream with babylights around front with balayage in back, alternating foil and teasy lights. Then I'll tone with a 9BV and 8PA." Umm, what? Don't get overwhelmed by the chemistry and math. You'll be just fine—I promise.

6. Salons can be gossipy and catty too. But let's be honest: no matter where you work, you'll always have someone who aggravates you, someone who's messy, someone who thinks they're better than everyone, or maybe someone who's always late or doesn't pull their weight. For me, I find working in a bigger salon with a lot of people is actually easier. We never have the same people in the break room, and we have all types of genders, ages, and talents. And if you pick a bigger and busier salon, you're all busy, so there is no time for drama. Sure, you'll have some downtime in the break room, but if you keep yourself busy with side work the drama usually stays away. You can always go work in your own studio suite by yourself, if you'd rather that. Some people find they love smaller salons, and that's cool too. Do you. Find your happy place. I personally love a big salon because I have so many people to learn from (young, old, new, veteran).

7. Occasionally, you will get an asshole client who you'd love to flip off. But then you have to check yourself and realize "the customer is always right." Remember: you're in the service industry. This is just the way the world turns—get over it. As long as you give a thorough consultation and explain all the possible results, all you can do is offer to fix it free of charge, because that is *your reputation* they're about to

smear over social media. Kill them with kindness and then go outside and scream.

8. If you're a booth renter, it gets more expensive the better you get. The more clients you have, the more color and products you buy. The better you are known, the more you'll have to stay on trend and have the best name-brand tools. Sometimes you must spend money to make money (highlight this phrase, for sure).

9. Your clothes will be ruined. Wear the damn apron.

10. Your nails will look like shit. Wear the damn gloves. You should see the way I hand money to cashiers; I tuck my nails in. It's embarrassing sometimes.

11. You'll be working in close quarters; bad-breath clients are a real thing. So are skin diseases and lice. Be prepared and be aware.

12. Once you get pretty good, you will never have a full lunch all in one sit-down again. Your bites will be in small doses and spread-out intervals, and your food will be stupid cold. Bring food that's still good cold and at room temperature; you'll rarely get time to eat a full hot meal all in one sitting. Maybe it's just me, but cold fries are gross.

13. Oh, this one sucks. You have to keep up with your taxes. I'm legit going to have to write an entire book on this. It is so unfair that some of the most artistic people go through schooling, and no one ever teaches us how to do our expenses and taxes. Get ready. If you can, get a CPA.

14. Your bladder will become very ignored. Going to the potty when you want to is a thing of the past.

15. When you come to a point in your stylist life where you think it's a good time to go up on your prices, you will have to have a super awkward discussion with all your clients, even the long-term ones. Unless you're like me and you just stick a sign up on your mirror—very sleek and professional looking, of course—that states something like "Due to the increase in pricing of our products and supplies by our distributors, starting April 1, my prices will also increase to reflect this change." Then I made a chic brochure with all my new pricing in a little holder under that note. What I really wanted the sign to say was "I'm getting super awesome and my books are full and I've invested a lot of time and money to get to this point, and I spend a crapload of money on this expensive color and product, so pay up if you'd like to stay in my chair." Kidding (a little).

PRO TIP

Have to miss work for sickness, maternity, or a broken bone? Some of our stylists get a supplemental insurance plan that will pay them when they're out for things like that. It can be as cheap as $35 a month. When you get to a good spot in your career, look into it.

16. If you're a booth renter, when you don't work, you don't get paid. You're sick? Oh well, if you miss work, now you're gonna be broke too. It's a pain to miss work once you're a successful hairstylist. If I'm not feeling well, I have to sit there in my bed and call or text all my clients and play *Tetris* with my schedule. I have to either put them with other stylists or plan to work extra late when I get back to fit them all in.
    - You have to make sure your formulas are explained just right, and they know your exact technique to perform so your client is happy with that other stylist they had to go to while you were out.

- The preparation a stylist must do to miss a day of work is strenuous. Calling each client and asking if they'd rather come another day (which may mean working until 9:00 p.m. because your books are already full and you have no where to put them), or go with another stylist (and then you have to give that super descriptive formula I spoke of above and hope that they execute your plan so that you don't come back to a mess of that client's hair at their next appointment.
- You're doing all of this calling and descriptive formulas usually from a sick bed or an insane morning when you've decided to take that day off—not fun. Last-minute sick days are so crappy to organize.

17. Your friends and family will always expect discounts. The worst is when they ask you over for dinner and then ask you to bring your shears for a service too. "Um, no, Sharon. You're an accountant. I don't ask you over for supper and ask you to bring your calculator to my house to do my taxes." Start this rule from the beginning—never bring your tools home. And don't give discounts (except for the handful who are very close to you).

18. When you get busy, you'll never have time to color your hair.
    - I literally highlight my own hair in my bathroom at home every three months or so. It's pathetic, actually. You feel bad asking someone else to do it on their day off as well. Our stylists are amazing, and I know they'd do my hair if I asked them. With my crazy schedule, sometimes it's just easier to do at home. The other stylists schedule time during the day or their off days to do each other's hair. There's a saying, "You know you have a good stylist when they never have time to do their own color and hair." That's not really a fact, but I can definitely see the truth in it.

Alyssa Nezat has been booth renting for almost fifteen years. She makes her own rules, she's her own business, and she's made a huge name for herself in our city.

Every industry has crap parts. I don't think ours are that bad. But to each their own. As for the money stuff I was talking about in chapter 1, let me go into a little more detail.

CRAP MONEY PART WHILE IN SCHOOL

1. Maybe you are blessed, and money is not much of an issue for you, but all in all, it sucks having to be in school and not have an income.

2. Some cos schools are Monday–Friday; some are Tuesday–Saturday. Either way, they take up most of your time. But I guess it is the same for college students too. Some people let loose because they're not in high school anymore and go buck wild and party, and they end up skipping class. This makes their graduation day further away and makes their days of being broke even longer, which in turns makes some people quit cos school early to go and make some money.

3. It's hard to have a job on top of being in school all day, especially when you get to the end of cos school, when you're on your feet the entire day in the salon portion of school.

4. Most of you will get some type of loan to go to school, whether it be from that school or a bank. Sometimes this slips students' minds. So that little bit of money you may make in your first salon will most likely be going toward your loan. Don't forget about this part—that's why you need that backup plan to make some side money.

5. Basically, what I'm saying is that you're going to be broke and tired. Expect it and plan for it. Good news: everyone in college is in the same predicament, so don't feel too sorry for yourself.

CRAP MONEY PART IF YOU WORK IN A COMMISSION SALON

To clarify, a commission salon is where you have a boss who actually owns the salon, and you're an employee. He or she will create all the rules and usually pay for absolutely anything. They pay for your products (usually), tools (usually), and all your color. They pay for your towels, washing detergent, advertisement, receptionist—everything. With this luxury, however, you only get a percentage of all the services you do. They also control when you have to work.

1. So now you have a boss with rules, who tells you when you must work, even if you sit there all day with no clients.

2. You will also start out with pretty much zero clientele—this is common in any type of salon you work in, though, so don't get too disheartened.

3. Sometimes they *might* pay you a small hourly wage, but mostly you only get a percentage of the services you perform.

4. When you start out at a commission salon, you are obviously at the bottom of the totem pole, so you will get the lowest percentage of your services.
    - Example: A lot of commission salons will start you out at making 35–40 percent of the services you perform.

PRO TIP

If you are a booth renter, get a business bank account. Shoot, just put $200 in it. But when you get your first paying client, make sure it goes to that account. And then any purchase you make that you can write off, use that business account. Do not use cash—just use that debit card. Then, for taxes, just print out your tax statements. You won't have to save all your receipts! You'll thank me later. If you at least start this step, you're starting on a good foot.

So, if you do a woman's haircut and charge forty dollars, you will only get sixteen dollars from that service.

- As you get better and fuller books, your percentage of what you get from services will increase.

5. Your new boss might make you stay nine to five. You may only have three clients in that entire time period. After that, you'll likely need a night job to make ends meet and pay for your everyday expenses, along with your new school loan they will be expecting you to start paying.

6. No matter how much money you make, you only get to keep a percentage of it. This entire commission idea is perfect in some areas, especially when it is practically impossible to open your own salon because the cost to lease is expensive. Sometimes commission salons are your best salons. Do your homework. Go and be a spy in your area and see which salons are your favorite and if they're commission or booth rent.

THERE ARE SOME BENEFITS TO COMMISSION SALONS

Before I completely scare you off, there are some positives about working in a commission-based salon:

1. The stress of running a business is, for the most part, off your shoulders. They take care of the insurance, taxes, and other aspects that you rarely think about when owning an LLC. You just show up and do your work.

2. That up-front cost of all your color and products—and sometimes tools—is something you won't have to worry about. The owner takes care of all the purchasing, products, supplies and all other items you may need to take care of your client services.

3. You're more likely to be at work more often, since being a booth renter

allows you to take off when you want, which is sometimes done way too much by booth renters, and it entices them to block off their schedules excessively.

4. Your personal taxes are a lot easier if you're a commission worker.

5. After a while of doing great services and staying booked, your salon owner might up your commission percentage.

6. Commission salons are a great place to start since you'll most likely have zero clientele. And if your area has a booth rental salon you'd like to move to, most of your clientele will move with you if they like you.

CRAP MONEY PART IF YOU WORK IN A BOOTH-RENTAL SALON

A booth rental salon is where someone owns a salon. That salon owner (who is like a landlord of an apartment complex) has a few things they pay for, like the receptionist, towels, and cleaning supplies. Then a booth renter comes along and rents a station from this owner. While doing this, this renter gets to keep *all* the money from their services after they've paid their monthly booth rent. But this booth renter will pay for their own products, tools, and color on top of their rent. It's like renting an apartment. You are responsible for everything in your apartment.

1. So now you're practically your own boss. That's pretty sweet, but being your own boss means having responsibility for *all* your expenses.

2. Like I just explained in the definition of a *booth-rental salon*, you'll have to pay for your products, your tools, your foil, all your color and developer, and, of course, your rent.
    - For example, in Lafayette, Louisiana, at our salon, a full-booth renter pays $765 a month, and I personally spend about $500 a month on products, color, and supplies. Now

think about how much I need on top of this to pay my house note, car note, groceries, insurance, gas, etc.

3. The other crap part about being a booth renter is taxes! Ugh, this is literally most stylists' yuckiest part.

4. And, of course, the "duh" crap part—your starting clientele. In this book, I give some tips on how to improve this area, but honestly, it does suck at first. Just have faith. This part doesn't stay crap for long if you've got that hustle and hunger.

THERE ARE SOME BENEFITS TO RENTING A BOOTH

1. Besides the up-front cost of all your color and products, the obvious benefit to being a booth renter is you get to keep every penny of the service you performed.

2. You're pretty much your own boss now and usually don't have to ask permission to leave early or take off certain days.

3. Being that you're your own boss, you can pick and choose the services you offer and how much time you'd like to block off to perform them.

4. Even though you must purchase all your products and color, in most salons, you'll get to choose your favorite brands.

5. Once your career starts blossoming, you'll have an opportunity to make your booth rent for the entire month in two to three days in some areas.

Again, all careers have crap parts. Just be prepared for the ones I've talked about, instead of being shocked and discouraged by them. You've got this, friend.

SIDEBAR *WITH* MCKENZIE TURLEY

McKenzie Turley has a little advice for cosmetology students:

"Use your time in cosmetology school as a dress rehearsal for the 'real show,' when you get your license and go to work in a salon. Lean on your instructors in the beginning as you are learning, but push yourself to start formulating and creating your process on your own. This is the time to begin thinking for yourself so you won't be thrown off when you step into the salon the first day. Also, use your time in school to practice good communication with your guests. They may be a guest of your school, but as soon as they sit in your chair, they are yours. Make sure to establish good consultation habits now so your flow will be easy and thorough once you're on your own."

@hair.extension.queen

5 SNEAKY, SNEAKY

Let's start you off on a good foot in school. Let's secretly get you ahead of the game.

Let's be real here: This is going to sound mean. Once you get into your classroom on your first day of school, look around. A small percentage of your classmates will make it. I can think back to all the students in school at the same time I attended—classes before and after me—and I can only think of about three who are actually in the hair industry. Most of the cosmo students think it's just about the school, the book, the easy-peasy stuff you do in class and on the school salon floor. They seem to believe they'll breeze through school and get to a salon and start making a lot of money. They'll get cocky in school, and some get bored—they think, *Oh, this is easy*, and start missing school, going out on school nights, coming in late, etc. Don't let their sloppiness rub off on you. Believe me, it's extremely contagious. Here's what you'll see:

PRO TIP

Start stalking the big-dog stylists in your area. Check their work. Find someone to look up to. Book a shampoo and style with them and build a little relationship (sneaky, sneaky).

1. Students get bored with the monotonous everyday schedule of cosmetology school—morning lecture, mannequin work, break, study, mannequin work, lunch, afternoon lecture, study, or mannequin work. When you get further up, you start adding salon floor at your school, and you have people coming in for cheap services. Each service takes forever because your teacher must approve and watch every step.
    - Ignore the bored students. You'll be bored, too, I promise. But here's your first trick: do extra homework. Seriously, be the dork, be the nerd—embrace that shit. Watch hair videos, makeup videos, follow the big names in the industry on social media. If you're really feeling fancy, at least start practicing those same updos or makeup on mannequins or friends. Definitely stay away from the shears or color until you have a better hold on that.
    - And best of all, keep it quiet. Of course, lots of these people are your friends, but remember: they're also your competition. To this day, I'll still go on my fellow stylists' Instagram pages and see which celebrity stylists they follow to make sure I'm not left out or missing out on some new technique or hair secret. The reason I say to keep this on the hush is you don't want any naysayers from school who may discourage you with their dream-crushing comments, like, "You trying to be teacher's pet?" or "Don't you have a life?" Some students are there for the cute stuff and just think they'll magically make it in the industry—you're not that person. You'll be secretly pushing forward and beyond them while they're not looking. Do the extra!

2. You'll see the lazy ones start to show themselves. They'll start missing because they have hangovers or they have cramps or they didn't sleep much the night before. It's so easy to fall into this group. Most students are usually coming straight from high school, where there was structure.

Now is their first chance at adulting and disciplining themselves, and the slackers quickly show their faces. If they end up finishing school or even at all, these are usually the ones in the real salon who block off days on their schedule to go shopping and whatnot and end up getting out of the industry because they're not making enough money.

- Here's your chance. This is where the disciplining yourself starts to build. Give yourself two excuses to miss school: fever and funerals. *Do not let yourself miss.* Trust me, you'll be so pissed when your projected graduation day passes you by because of the days of school you missed. Muscle up, hustle up. I believe I may have been the only student in my class who actually finished school on the day I was supposed to. It was hard—trust me. I even got married while I was in school and still finished on time.

3. You'll start seeing some basic work. They'll do work just to pass a section. These are usually the ones who will do the same in the salon. These are usually the ones who never take those extra classes to further themselves in the industry and the ones who get stuck in their comfortable ways and get left behind as hungry stylists pass them by.
    - Go beyond. Not for the teachers, necessarily, but for you. Throw a little sparkle on that assignment. Watch some extra videos on social media—do it better. *You're only as good as the training you do when no one is looking.*

PRO TIP

Start getting your hair done where you want to work. Start planting the seed. Dress to impress when you go there. Play it cool, mention you're in school, play with the pics of your work on your phone as you're getting your hair done. Make them ask about you.

- If the assignment is to do a prom updo, you do the best damn prom updo that school has ever seen, even if the student on the side of you does a messy top bun just to get it over with. Don't let them pee pee on your parade. Be over the top and don't apologize for it.

4. Some will be your typical social media ding-dongs who post everything they did over the weekend—their keg stands, their kissy-faces, their parties—don't be them. You're above that.
   - Start a hair or makeup page account immediately. *Start right now.* Even if you haven't even gotten in school yet, or maybe you just started, start a page now. You don't have to have any followers; just go play with an account name. Make sure it is *just* your professional work—no lame selfies. I keep Facebook for friends and family and Instagram for work.
   - On that note, watch some videos on how to make your pics and videos better. As an owner, we rarely hire a stylist right out of school at our salon (notice I said "rarely"; we've done it three times in nine years). But in the rare case we do, my business partner does her—what we call—FBI work. She hits up their social media page. Trust me, pics tell us everything. You can decipher between an average student and a stand-out student. I can tell you that we have single-handedly not hired people because of their cheesy, lame, or subpar work on their social media pages. If their work on social media looks mediocre, they most likely will not be working at our salon.
   - Our stylists send us pics all the time of their work to post on our salon page. But if the pic isn't up to par, my business partner won't post it. You better make sure your work is on point and that picture is amazing. I really mean it when I say to research how to fix your pics. And please don't use filters; I'm talking about blurring the backgrounds, the angle in

which you take it, the position in which you put your client.

5. Now let's make this fun from day one for you. Look around your class, and in the first few days find your competition. After the first few easy mannequin assignments, you'll be able to see who you're working against. Yes, I know, cosmetology school is not a competition. But the salon industry is. Our salon may be friendly with the other salons in our city—most of them are our great friends. But when you get down to it, though it may be friendly, we are in competition.
   - Find those one or two people right there in the beginning days in your class. Let them be your motivation. When they miss a day or two, you'll already be graduating before them and gaining clients and working in a big salon before them. When you see their work, do yours better. Remember: research if you must.
   - I remember this from a friend of mine who started cos school with me. She was so cool, tatted up, pink hair—I just vibed with her. Later on, she became a rep for a few big-brand salon products. She came into my salon one day to talk about her product line and told me that back in the first week in hair school, after she saw my work, she knew I was her competition. She said I always kept her motivated because she always wanted to do better than me. I never knew she thought of me that way. That stuck with me. It was a big compliment, but I thought that was such great advice.

Pretend you're a secret agent in school. Be supercool, maybe even quiet, but be killing it on the side. Stay so far ahead of them that when you graduate, you've taken off like a rocket so far ahead of them that they can't see you anymore. Keep your standards higher than theirs. And by standards I mean:

- Never be late.
- Never miss school.

- Always have your hair and makeup done. Even though it's just school, you're building your brand and creating great habits.
- Create a good reputation. When salons have an open chair and no new fresh résumés coming in, they will call the local schools to ask about their best students. Be their best student.
- Keep your work the best in the class, or at least try. If it's not, still be humble and inspired by others' work.

Don't be cocky; be inspired. Don't look down on their work. Ever. Take notes, see what you like, how you would improve theirs, what you don't like, but be inspired at the same time. You'll do this for the rest of your life—judge other people's hair. Whether it be in the checkout line at the grocery store or sitting at a football game in the stands and looking at the back of fans' hair. You'll check the color and style they have and start fixing it in your mind. I'm constantly imagining people I see with different hair. I won't remember their name, but I will remember that cowlick in the front of their hairline that I want to teach them how to style.

John Paul Dejoria, cofounder of John Paul Mitchell Systems, says, "Successful people do all the things that unsuccessful people don't want to do."[*] He spoke so much truth in that one quote. No one *wants* to do extra work, and not many people like to spend their free time doing anything other than chilling. This man is a billionaire for a reason. Be a go-getter; don't be lazy. In the book *Business Fundamentals: Connecting to My Future*, they further explain John Paul Dejoria's quote by saying, "He's talking about the important but seemingly little things that lead to a big career. Things like practicing the same skill again and again, until it becomes second nature. Being the first to arrive and the last to leave. Providing exceptional service to every guest, every time. Asking for referrals. Following up. Keeping your station clean. Looking and acting like a confident professional, both in person and online."[†] That's the real grind you must obtain.

---

[*] Claybaugh et al., *Business Fundamentals*, 1.

[†] Claybaugh et al., *Business Fundamentals*, 3.

I titled this chapter "Sneaky, Sneaky" because sometimes when you do the "extra" and you tell people about it, you're made fun of and called "nerdy." I don't want you to get discouraged; I want you to be secretly killing the game before you even get out of school. The more of the things you do in this chapter, the less time you'll spend "poor" when you get your first job. Set yourself up for success secretly; don't give away your upper hand. Observe, kick ass quietly, and keep those high standards for yourself. You're quietly setting yourself up to be a badass.

Lance Chouest did his sneaky homework in school and pulled the right strings. I had never hired an assistant before. He came and spoke with me before he even graduated, and with a little name-dropping from one of my clients, he became my first assistant. After three months, his books were full for weeks out.

SIDEBAR *WITH* **LARISA LOVE**

Larisa Love on how to get ahead in school:

"How to get ahead of the rest of the kids in school is really to think outside the box and say yes to everything. Just really be an artist and create your own journey along the way. Yes, it's great to know the fundamentals of everything they're teaching you. But honestly, make your own step into this world, into your career, by becoming the artist *you* want to be. So whatever it is you want to learn, go at it 100 percent. If you want to specialize in something, go at it 100 percent, because you never know what you love until you try it all out. Then truly get into what you want to specialize and run with it."

@Larisadoll

6 BADASS TOOLBOX

Your toolbox holds your superpower—your magic. Start building that sucker ASAP.

Most of your schools have a starter kit you'll get when you sign up. Make sure you get a list of what's in there. Depending on your school, some of it's good, and some of it's crap. If you are planning to surpass all your classmates and end up at one of the best salons in your area, you can't be showing up with rinky-dink tools. Start getting ahead of the game. Now is the time to be a penny-pincher and ask for certain gifts for holidays. Get ahead of the game and start building your badass toolbox. Start with your basics, but

> "No matter which aspect of this industry interests you most, as a beauty, nails, skin, or barbering professional, you are fundamentally a craftsperson. And like any other craft, such as painting, sculpting, or jewelry designing, you need the right tools to produce and promote your product."
> —*Business Fundamentals: Connecting to My Future*

* Claybaugh, *Business Fundamentals*, 90

make them legit. A cool trick is to go to your "goal" salon, make a hair appointment, and ask that stylist about their favorite tools. Go snooping. Go to a few of the best salons in your area—just get a brow wax or a shampoo or style—and ask the same thing! Also, for birthdays or holidays, ask for one tool—if you're lucky enough to have people to give you gifts like that!—for each time, and that will help you get to your badass-toolbox goal. Once you're in school, you can usually go to your local professional beauty supply store, and they'll let you buy at cost if you can prove you're in hair school.

1. Get yourself an amazing blow-dryer. Right now, I love the Paul Mitchell Neuro Halo Dryer. It has speed, heat, and ion settings, and so much more. It's at least $200, but it's one of the best investments you can make. This one is just my choice. Do your homework and pick one you like—preferably, a brand your goal salon uses. Some people like the Dyson hairdryer, to each their own. I once was a guest artist at a cosmetology school and did a blowout after the color technique I showed them. This homegirl forgot her blow-dryer and had to use the school's blow-dryer. OMG, it was the worst blowout I've ever done. I was so embarrassed. They didn't even have concentrator blow-dryer attachments, and my model had big ol' frizzy hair. My armpits were sweaty; I felt so stupid. Lesson learned: your tools have a big role in your outcome.

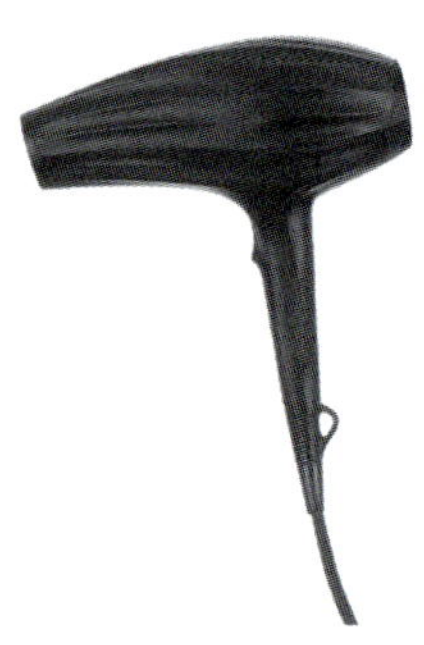

2. Next, get an amazing flat iron. I prefer 1" (and again, the Paul Mitchell Neuro Flat Iron). Mine has a smart chip in it that can run on your home computer. It checks its temperature fifty times a second so that you never get cold spots. It has an automatic thirty-minute shutoff and all sorts of cool tricks. Once you get a good one, also start practicing curling hair with a flat iron.

3. Get a 1" curling iron before anything. With this one, just make sure it's a great brand. Try to get titanium metal, if they have it. I have curling irons and wands in all shapes and sizes, but the 1" curling iron is what I use most. Sometimes this one is all you need, if you learn that it just depends on the width and length of your section as to which type of curl you'll get—tight, beachy, wavy.
   - After you get all these tools mentioned in this section, get other sizes of curling irons. Example: I have a .75" for updos, where I like to curl their hair and brush out before I pull it back. This way their hair looks wavy going back into the updo.
   - I also have a 1.25", 1.50", and a 1.75" curling iron—you'd be surprised that I actually use all of them for different curls I want, for different techniques I use, and for different types of hair I do.

4. Get a good set of professional clippers and trimmers. Again, this is a good one to ask your stylist. Make sure it comes with all the guards, etc. I personally like the cordless trimmers.

5. Find yourself a good type of shears. Mine are $1,000. My first pair out of school was $350.
   - For the shears, this is another one you may want to ask your personal stylist and the stylists around them.
   - You can also go and stalk some celebrity stylists and see what they use.
   - Don't stress about shears though. You can definitely use the ones they give you in school for a while. Wait until you're making enough money for yourself in the field first, or wait until someone wants to gift them to you.
   - And if you keep your shears sharpened—we have a guy who comes by the salon a few times a year to sharpen ours—they'll last you a long time.

Now start playing with products. If your mind is pretty set on a salon you'd like to shoot for, start playing with the products they primarily use—Paul Mitchell, Kevin Murphy, Oribe, Aveda, or maybe they don't have a particular brand. Research top celebrity stylists on social media and see which products they're using in their videos—not exactly the ones they are promoting, because sometimes they're just getting paid a lot to push it, and they don't necessarily use that product.

The basics:

- Four hairsprays—get a strong one, a flexible one, one for texture, and one for frizz.
- Dry shampoo—you can also play with the colored ones for brunettes or blondes.
- Leave-in conditioner—I use one on *every* client and practically demand they buy one. Some of that hair has been on their head for two or more years, so that midshaft down needs some extra lovin'.

This is another one of our veteran stylists, Tina Aucoin. She's a genius at blowouts. It truly sets apart an established stylist from a newer one.

- Volumizer or root spray—if your client needs volume, most have panthenol in it that expands the hair follicle when heat from your blow-dryer hits it.
- Smoothing product—find your favorite for before the blowout and after the blowout. Not all clients need this, but the ones who do *need* it badly.
- Heat protectant—if you don't spray this on dry hair before using any hot tools, you're legit frying hair. Tell them the same; this one is a must.

Honestly, all the other products are lagniappe to help them fix their hair at home the way you could probably do it without any products. Those products are there to help them achieve the goal you want them to walk around town with showing off your work. There are also products you need to make yourself familiar with for special cases, like dandruff, thinning hair, frizzy hair, curly hair, updo hair, and hair of all ethnicities. Make yourself versatile—know all types of hair and the perfect product to fix it. Start building your product arsenal and your toolbox to set you on the right foot to start out!

Once you are in school, you can usually start shopping at the local salon industry stores—the ones only salon professionals are allowed to shop at. Start going and buying a product or two and using them on yourself to see which ones are your favorites. You'll get that licensed stylist discount. Just make sure you buy a quality brand tool. That way, it lasts for years. I've had some tools for

PRO TIP

When you get established, you can have two of every tool so you'll never have to pack for bridal parties or travel event updos or makeup. It's a pain in the ass to work a full day behind the chair only to have to pack everything up and make sure you have everything for a wedding or event the next day. And then, when you come back to work, having to unpack everything kind of sucks too.

over fifteen years, so it's not something you'll buy very often. So, when you do purchase one, spend the money and buy the good ones.

If you'd like to be bougie, go and get one of the coolest bags for your tools. I have a roller bag that keeps my makeup at the bottom and hair stuff at the top. This is perfect when you have weddings or must travel for a service. This is obviously something you can get way later, but if you have people who want to get you gifts, invest in something like this.

Remember: you're trying to take off right after you graduate hair school, so prepping that toolbox is only going to push you further ahead of your peers and will keep you from having to fork up so much money right in the beginning at your new salon. But if this is something you're financially unable to do, don't stress. It's perfectly fine to use the tools you were given in hair school to start with. Shoot, they may even help you better perform in the future because you didn't have the luxury or all the fancy aspects of the expensive tools in the beginning. If you can create an amazing head of hair with barely anything, imagine what you'll be able to do when you have all the deluxe tools at your disposal.

Our receptionist, Chasity Viator, takes care of all our product sales. Product sales are free money in your pocket from the commission, and it makes your client's hair look good weeks after their appointment.

7 SOCIAL MEDIA = BEST FRIEND

So, if cosmo school sounds like it's about to be your thing, and you're gonna make the jump, start by cleaning up your social media. Like I said, I co-own one of the biggest salons in our city, and I still creep on cosmetology school students' pages. We rarely hire right out of school, but every once in a while we get frisky and see a shining star in one of the cosmo schools around here, and we'll snatch them up.

Go look at your Facebook page. Personally, I would decide right now to reserve one social media outlet for friends and family only, and another outlet for just work. For example, I keep Facebook just for my friends and family—I rarely post work pics there—mainly because I have pics of my children on there, and I don't want creepers looking at my kids. Plus, when my kids get older, I don't want them to be pissed at me for showing the world their personal memories and photos.

PRO TIP

Before you post anything, check it and edit your wording—step away from the post before you post it. Be careful and strategize your posts. Make them amazing.

PRO TIP

Even if you don't add any followers yet, start that Insta page now. Watch some TikTok videos of how to take good pics—lighting, transitions, etc.—and that should help. Do not add crap pics to your page. A salon owner who's about to hire you will go straight to your page. If I see some old funky curls not brushed out, bad styling, or plain-Jane hair, I will scroll on past you. I've taken classes on bios and highlights, so if you ever have questions or need advice, hit me up on social media.

Then I keep all my work on Instagram. That way, when you go to my Insta page, you won't see all sorts of personal moments—you'll mainly just see my work in hair. I let anyone follow that page, and I don't put my kids on there. But even if you don't have kids, it looks much more organized for a potential client to go visit your work page and see just work. It looks much more professional, and it shows you take your job seriously.

I know you don't have much work to show right now, but my point is, start your organizing. Pretend you do it the way I do it. Go now and start an Instagram page, even if you have no work to post, and get your profile the way you want it. Get a profile pic ready, etc. Even start your first pic with something about starting cosmo school. Edit your bio, etc.

1. You don't even have to add any friends right now to your page. Just start slowly posting badass pics to get a cool page going.

2. Make sure each pic is legit. Make sure it is lit correctly, and do not use filters. Every stylist knows this trick, and we make fun of other stylists who do it.

3. Don't make boring comments about each pic; make it catchy. And don't make every single post a lengthy story, no one likes to read a whole bunch anymore.

4. Some people have themes to their pages. You can look at some of our

stylists' pages and see a theme they have going. It's hard to explain, but they just all flow when you look at all their pics together. If you press the Reels button on our salon page (@thecuthousesalon), our amazing receptionist, Chasity Viator, titled each one so it looks cool and cohesive.

5. There are pro stylist pages that actually show you how to pose your models. They show you the weird positions to put them in that catches that money shot.

6. No subpar work here. Take a crapload of pics just to pick one amazing one.

7. I think the magic number at this point in time is eleven hashtags on Instagram. Of course, this could change. Research their algorithms—find what makes posts circulate. Instagram also likes when you use their tools they provide, like polls and questions.

PRO TIP

Start playing around with a simple logo. Keep it simple and picture it on all your clients' photos. Message me; I know a few websites that do a pretty great job at making logos. They compete with each other for your logo!

8. Make sure to reply to each comment on all your posts, even if you don't know the person. It's polite, it shows you stay active on your page, it shows you appreciate the comments, and it makes others more prone to comment on your future posts. Try to comment more than four words (not counting emojis). This also is supposed to help in the algorithms of your post circulating.

9. Find the best lighting in the room for your client pics. Indirect light or shaded areas outside are best.

10. Blur out your backgrounds; they have apps for this. If you can't find them, message me, and I'll shoot you a few.

11. If you have a logo or watermark, put that on every client pic so your work is less likely to be stolen and used elsewhere.

12. You can smooth out clients' wrinkles and zits if you feel you should—you didn't work on their face; you just want them to feel comfortable—but *never change their hair*. Again, filters are obvious and a big no-no.

Start filming and photographing everything. Play with apps and reels and get good at it. This is free advertising, and if you build a page before you get out of school, you're already ahead of the others.

13. Put your city and state and as much valuable info you can in your bio. This makes you easy to find. Once you're more established, you're welcome to message me, and I can help you with that. You'll add all your important certifications, your school or salon, all of it. But don't make it cluttered—make it clean and readable.

14. Start your Instagram highlights (those circles underneath your bio). You can have highlights like "before and afters," "client reviews," "about me." Remember: Instagram loves when you use their tools.

Your social media should not have party nights, political views, mean stuff, etc. Keep it professional. You're selling yourself now and are trying to reach a variety of people—different genders, liberals, conservatives, ages, *everybody*. Don't shut yourself off from a certain group of people because of the things you post. Don't turn them away because you were twerking at the club. Keep your social media professional. Time to be an adult now. Keep your crazy hush-hush.

Social media is free advertising (well, unless you "boost" your post. You can also message me on how to do this). If you become comfortable and professional in your post making, this will definitely grow your clientele. Stay relevant and delete your posts and clean up your page from time to time. I just recently scrolled all the way down to the bottom of my Instagram to find my old post, and I was downright embarrassed. It looked like a twelve-year-old posted those. You tend to forget how quickly this industry evolves and shifts from certain styling techniques.

Start thinking of your social media name now and get to work. You'll be putting this name on your business cards, so don't make it stupid like @sharonlikeskegstands or anything dumb like that. Get ahead of everyone in your class now, even if you haven't even entered school yet.

This is Cami Ezernack. On Instagram, she is @hairxcami. She's badass at taking great client pics. She makes sure she allots at least five minutes after her appointments to take good pics. I even make her take some of my after pics for me sometimes.

8 WHY ARE YOU THEIR WIZARD?

Now, I know you're just thinking about getting into school right now, or maybe you've signed up or just started, but I need you to get into a certain mindset. Do you realize how many stylists are in your area? Honestly, do you know that number? What makes you so special that your client picks you? What makes you their own personal wizard? What's going to make a client come to your cosmo school or salon and start asking specifically for you? They can find so many other stylists in your area, or even in your salon, who can do the same thing as you. What makes you so important? Start establishing this mind frame while you're in school. You'll start being able to get on the school salon floor soon in your cosmetology training. Take advantage of it. Make those clients *ask* for you because you're better than the others.

1. Make their hair listen to you. I know that sounds stupid, but boss that thing around. Dig into it. Know it.
   - I can't remember my client's last name sometimes, but I remember exactly where their cowlicks are without even touching their hair. I remember where their moles are. I remember their crazy-ass hairlines. I remember it all. Truly know it—make it your project. You'll surprise them next

time when you say, "Your hair wants to do this, so I'm going to do this this time." They'll know they can trust you, and they're not just another client in your chair.

- If you want to be super nerdy, make notes of it. Once you get into a salon, you'll most likely have access to their salon program, where you can save their formulas and important information. Since you don't have this quite yet, start a notebook. Write things like "certain product smells bother her," or "don't cut his cowlick in the back too short." The fact that you remember little bits of information about your clients will impress them.

2. Make their first consultation the longest one they've ever had. You are now their "caring hair wizard." Don't just tell them to show you one inspiration pic. Sometimes that's bad, because they'll show you some celebrity's hair that obviously has been photoshopped or has extensions, and your client has like nineteen hairs on their head. Make them show you three or so pics and ask questions about each one, narrowing down what you think it is they "actually" like about those pics. Here's another trick: make them show you what they *don't like* too.
   - Once they've shown you a few pics, actually point to parts of the pic and ask them to tell you the exact parts they like about the pics. You may not get this advice at first, but you will eventually. Example: You may see the black roots in balayage pics, and all they are really wanting is those color blond tips. So now you've gone too dark on their roots, their bill is way higher than they wanted, it's a bad grow out, etc. Make them *literally* point to the parts of the pic they like.
   - This is so funny, but it works every time. When they show you a pic of a style they really want, cover the model's face with your thumb. Tell them, "Now I want you to picture this hair on your face. Really imagine it." Then tell them,

"Now picture this hair after it ran sixteen errands that day and then went home and cleaned their garage. What do you think that hair would look like then? Can you picture that on yourself?" A lot of times they see the bomb-ass makeup and the full blowout the stylist gave the model in the pic; they never picture their face under that same hair after they have styled it themselves. It's hilarious.

- *Write down their formulas.* Be so detailed that it sounds like you are explaining it to a kindergartner. Everyone makes fun of my clients' formula cards and how detailed they are. But let me tell you how many times they've gotten me out of sticky situations, including emergency situations in which I had to miss work and someone had to take my client, or a past formula that didn't work, so I make sure not to use it again. I personally always liked having a little box and using index cards with those little alphabetical organizers in it. I never liked having a formula book; it's just a personal preference. But over the past few years, I started using our salon's scheduling program to save all my formulas. This is a great source; however, make sure wherever you work that it's in their contract that if you ever leave that salon you can have access to your clients' formulas when you leave. I can't stand when salons treat stylists who are leaving like criminals. It's in our contract that when you leave our salon you can take every bit of client info and your formulas with you. Once they tell me that they've gotten all the information they need, I ask them if it's OK to delete them from our system.

3. Please do not do the "Surprise! How do you like your hair?" at the end of your appointment. A true hair wizard will teach their magical ways and educate their client on how to style their masterpiece at home. Walk and talk them through it. Oh man, I cannot stand when stylists

turn their clients sideways for most of the appointment, especially when blow-drying after they shampoo because they're scared themselves of what it's going to look like. Then they turn their chair around for the client to see the end result in the mirror, and they're put on the spot. If they didn't get to talk with you through the appointment, how do you know for sure they're getting what they want? It's kind of like your aunt giving you a super weird sweater as a gift, and you must open it up in front of her. You get put on the spot with your reaction, so you say, "Oooooh, thaaaannnks." Don't put them in that situation.

- Have them pull their hair to the front and *show* you exactly where they want it cut. Sometimes they like the pic they show you, and you do exactly that, and they say you chopped their hair too short. If you ask before you cut, you've made it their problem, not yours.
- Show them how you want them to blow-dry it. I show them how to get volume, I show them how to section it, etc. Remember: they are your billboard! If they are not fixing their hair out in public, how is someone going to ask them where they got their hair done, because they loved it? They are the main reason you'll get new clients. Make sure they *know* how to fix it!
- The worst is when you do the "surprise" thing for brides, bridal parties, or any updos. My advice: fix the front first. It's the most important part. It's what they see in the mirror and what they'll see in pics at the event. Then work your way toward the back. Or, if you can't, at least discuss the front with them when you get to that point. There is nothing worse than having to do an updo all over again because they hate it.
- On some rare occasions, you might get a client who actually wants to be surprised. You can, of course, do that, but I would still walk and talk them through the important

This is Michelle Domingue. She gives the most thorough consultations. Trust me, I'm a few chairs down from her, and I hear them all. She asks what kind of water they have, how much they style their hair, everything.

decisions, like length, etc. I'd also still talk them through how you're blow-drying and styling to make sure they know how to do the same at home.

4. Throw a little extra magic into their service to make them feel special and prove you're *their* wizard. Maybe it's a longer scalp massage. Maybe it's a quick side braid. Maybe you have an extra sample at your station to give them to try, or maybe treat them with a coffee that day because they're your first client of the morning. Sprinkle a little glitter on that appointment. Show them you're different than their last stylist.

Once you become their hair wizard, they may move away to another town but still drive to see you. This client drives from another state to see me. You form a bond and a trust that you don't feel like starting with anyone else.

5. Let them talk most of the time. Yes, you're their hair wizard, but show them that you care about them and what's happening in their lives as well. Ask them guided questions, like, "What do you guys have planned for this weekend?" Let *them* talk to you. Don't hog the appointment and talk about yourself and your problems so much that they feel like therapists. There will always be stylists around you who complain all day to their guests—about their baby daddies, day-care issues, lack of sleep, etc. It's exhausting, especially when the stylist next to you does this at every appointment, and you've heard the same complaining crap six times that day. Let your guests talk and guide them along the way.

6. Complete your wizardry by talking about the products you've specifically chosen for them and why. This is not because you want to sell to them—though that would be nice too—but because it'll help them at home style *your* work. You can even add, "I'm not trying to be a car salesman. I mean, use what you have at home first, but when you're done, come by and get this because I want your hair to always look good and be easy for you to replicate."

Always make them feel like *you* are their hair wizard. No one understands them or their hair like you. And if their relationships or appointments start getting "dull," it's time to shake things up a bit. Remember: there's always a stylist down the street who may be catching your client's eye on social media. Be their own personal hair wizard so that they always scroll on past that other stylist.

SIDEBAR *WITH* **STEPHANIE KOCIELSKI**

Stephanie's view on the many facets of the industry:

"There are so many facets to the hairstylist industry. You can be an educator; you can be an Instagram star. Whatever your goal is, find a mentor that you love their work and brand and start looking at the style of your page. Look at the content you're posting every day. By posting daily, you can see your talent grow not only as a stylist but as a photographer. Start to build your brand.

"You can also be a traveling guest artist for a manufacturer—this is what I love the most. Unlimited are the possibilities for your future, and there's no end to your talent. My favorite saying is, 'Bring your talent . . . but don't forget your responsibility' to people you serve, to yourself, to your family. Enjoy this career; it's the best, and I've been rocking it for forty years going strong! You, my friend, can manifest anything you wish."

@kocielski

9 WILL YOU GET BORED?

If you get bored in this industry, you're a moron. Kidding. This is one of the coolest jobs. It's artistic, it's social, it's creative, and it can bring in *so much money*. But that money does not just show up on your doorstep. Cosmetology is an art, with many facets and specialties. If one section doesn't speak to you, try walking in another path. The umbrella of cosmetology is insanely huge; you can pick one talent under it and perfect it or dabble in all of it.

Let's focus on the day-to-day routine of a new stylist. Your first main focus is to just break into the industry and make a name for yourself. You have to get your name spoken around town—that has to be your number-one goal. Let's say you've done all of the "sneaky, sneaky" things I've told you in the previous chapter while in school to get your foot in the door of the salon you've had your eyes on. Let's pretend you've finally made it into that salon. What do you do now? Do you just wait for clients to come through that door? Do you just cross your fingers and hope a little bird told someone to come and make an appointment with you? Um, negative, my friend. You're just starting the bored journey that every new stylist begins with—it's called the sit and wait. But I'd like you to approach those boring days with a different attitude. Plant some seeds to gain clients and gain a reputation as a team player.

1. Ask how the dang washer and dryer work and start washing and folding towels. Every single stylist in the industry has to do that; don't wait for someone to ask you to do it.

2. Ask the receptionist (if you have one) to teach you how to check people out, schedule appointments, answer the phone (to help them out while they're at lunch), organize the product shelves.

3. Walk around the surrounding area of the salon and visit shops, visit restaurants, and give them your personal business card with maybe a 20 percent discount written on the back of it.

4. Walk around the salon and ask stylists if you can video or take pics for social media for them—practice making reels and stories with amazing fonts and music. They'll love that because sometimes a stylist is just too busy to take their own client photos.

5. Ask a stylist if you can watch them as they perform a service, or volunteer to shampoo a client for them. They usually secretly love showing off or teaching someone new. Don't be scared to ask if you can observe.

6. Call friends to come in and give them an amazing service. Take longer with them, give them an amazing blow-out (this will show other clients you know what you're doing and other stylists that they can put their clients with you when their own books are too full). You better make dang sure to take as many pics of your work in those beginning days, because that's all you'll have to show on your own social media. Even if it's just a brow wax, you better take some "before and afters" of that service!

7. Offer to shampoo and style other stylists' hair to practice and get some tips from them (so many new stylists barely scrub heads with shampoo at the bowl, and their blow-outs are usually subpar. It's like

they're scared to get rough with a client). I often ask the new stylists if I can shampoo and blow out their hair to show them how I expect them to perform. The number-one complaint my personal clients give me when I let a new assistant shampoo their head is that it felt like the assistant was barely scrubbing, and the blow out was kind of "meh."

8. Those first few months (sometimes shorter, sometimes longer) can be brutally boring at the beginning. This is where the industry loses a lot of stylists because they're not making money and have to find another job that will give them a more stable income. Overcome this; be better.

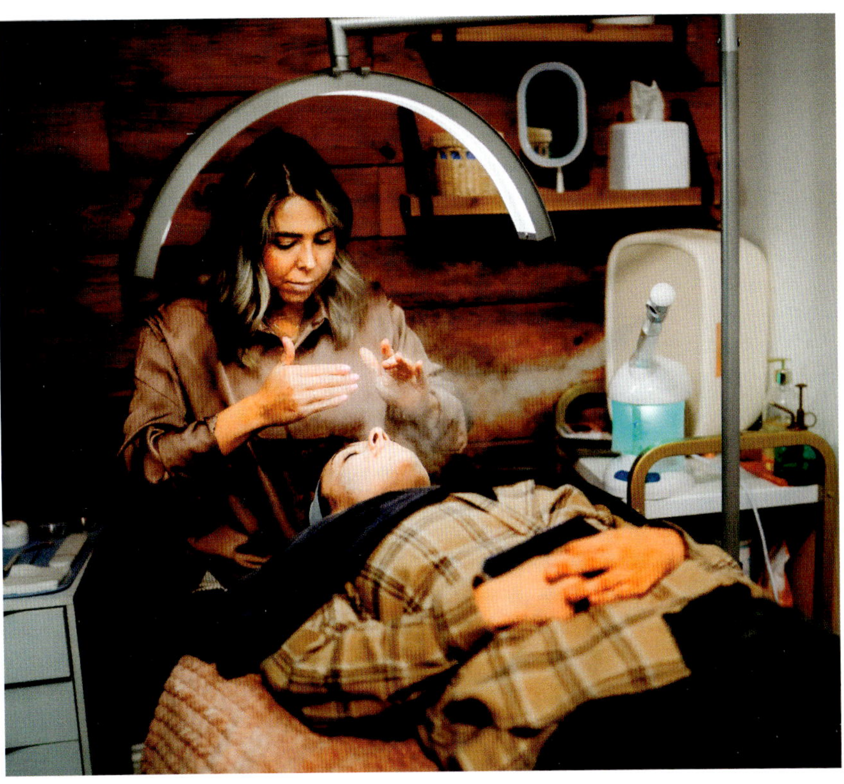

Our aesthetician, Destiny Bossier. This chick is a master at brows and does facials, lashes, teeth whitening, and tanning. Pick a path in cosmetology and become an expert.

Later on in this career, you may find you're getting bored with a particular service or facet of cosmetology. With that cosmetology license, you can do *so* much—you'll never be "stuck." When you're in school, you'll touch on everything—hair, makeup, nails, facials. Maybe when you're studying one of these subjects you might find that one of them stokes your fire a little more than the others. I've seen students go on to make *bank* after carving out a niche. Here are some examples:

1. I know a girl who learned to thread eyebrows after school, and she legit owns one of the bougiest eyebrow places in the fanciest part of my town, Lafayette, Louisiana. She *only* threads eyebrows, and you should see her place!

2. There's another cosmetology graduate who started a mobile spray-tanning business, and I'm pretty sure she's already hired other employees and bought another van. That is dope.

3. I know a guy, Josh Comeaux, who created his own hair-and-body oil. He used to work at our salon—look him up. He built his social media presence, pushed his product, and people all over the world are using it, especially on photo shoots. He went on to make Colormap. It's a sweet little notebook with shades of paper that are true to the color levels you can bleach hair. You then can put your fantasy colors on it to see what they'll actually look like. He then moved to California and pushed his product from there.

4. I've heard of a student realizing after school and getting her license that she didn't like working with people—ha-ha! Understandable, I guess—and now works for a popular pet-grooming business.

5. There's another girl in town who did hair for a while, went to a class on microblading eyebrows, got certified, and now has a huge studio that specializes in all things in facial tattooing.

6. I've seen people start their own mobile nail company and travel to homes doing amazing nails.

7. There's one girl who used to work in a morgue and did the hair and makeup of those who have passed away. As hard as that might be for some people, imagine the loved ones of that person and how good they must feel when the deceased looks so good to the visitors. Plus, she wasn't a talker and liked working "by herself."

8. I must brag about my Invisible Bead Extensions mentor and creator, McKenzie Turley. She got certified in all types of hand-tied extension methods and then went and nerded out and created her own method that is arguably the best method out there that has spread worldwide. She now owns her own product and extension line as well. She's a beast, and you need to follow her too. I have her on my "Inspo" section in the back, but she's worth mentioning twice—@hair.extension.queen. I'm currently a master in her IBE technique, and it is 100 percent my personal favorite service to perform.

9. One of our very own stylists, Maddie Grabert, started her own Instagram page in high school and started posting all the makeup services she was doing. She got a huge toolbox and started collecting all the best makeup. This girl has made so much money, and it's one of the first times we hired a student to come work for our salon right out of school—she's got hustle.

10. There are positions in which a licensed cosmetology professional can go into nursing homes and hospitals and actually reteach people how to care for their skin and hair and learn motor skills after accidents and setbacks.

11. There are also positions at hospitals and nursing homes to shampoo, style, and perm these patients to make themselves feel better!

12. There is also a chick I met who got pretty good at makeup, happened to cross paths with someone in the movie field, and now is a big movie-set makeup artist.

13. Just recently one of our very own stylists started dabbling in lashes. She's an insane makeup artist already. So we created some lash rooms, she gave up hair, and is now following her passion in lashes and makeup!

One of our stylists, Taylor Duhon, waxing her client. Some stylists choose to stay in the waxing subfield of cosmetology—some open waxing centers. The possibilities are endless.

Let's say you do hair for a while, love it, but get bored with it. Change it up! Go get certified in lash extensions. Shoot, start doing hair extensions. Dabble in nails or makeup or waxing. Cosmetology is an art. If you're bored, it's probably your work ethic that you should be looking at.

These are just some of the many paths you can take after going to cosmetology school. You can be a celebrity stylist, a movie-set artist, a funeral-home beautician—you've got so many options. Cosmetology is not a field in which you can get bored. You can travel the world with this career if you choose to. You can move anywhere, and a person just has to check your social media to see if you're any good. You can always learn a new technique in your specialty or veer off into another fork in the road and focus on one of the other elements in this world. Even if you stay in just hair, for example, you should see the things I've had to learn in the past ten years just to stay on top of my game that I did not learn in school—ombres, balayages, mullets, baby bangs, dreads, extensions, keratin treatments, new products, etc. If you get bored in this career, something's wrong with you (ha-ha, jk).

> **PRO TIP**
>
> Since there are so many other certifications you can add to your license (lashes, extensions, etc.), before or while you're in school, research which companies will let you get certified in their brand while you're in school. We had a stylist who was certified in a hand-tied extension method before he ever graduated.

You know how you can also be successful in this field and never get bored? If you are a social or caring person, you're going to kill it. Now let me not scare my quiet readers. We have a few very quiet stylists who are excellent at their jobs, and I believe their reputations have brought a clientele who complements them. A client once told me that she'd rather be with a stylist who didn't talk to her so she could relax—point taken, lady, point taken. No, but seriously, what I'm saying is this: If you love listening to people and their problems, issues, highs, lows, get ready—you're about to be in heaven. My clients are *my people*. I will go to bat for them any day. I had my first client pass away in 2021, and let me tell you, it hurt. She's been my homey for about six years. We knew so much about each other. When you lose a client, it hits different, I promise. My point is, get ready to get involved—that is, if you want to. You'll never get bored with the variety of clients who will rotate through your chair all day.

I get asked a lot: "Do you ever get tired of this?" My answer is no. I admit I have my favorite and not-so-favorite services I perform, but no, I don't get tired. In fact, when you get to where I am in the business, you can start dropping the services that don't tickle your fancy anymore. I always say that each client is like a new TV series. I don't get to watch a lot of TV—full appointment book, running a salon, husband, two kids, etc.—so each client is like a new TV show. And each time they sit in my chair is like a new episode. I get to catch up on their families, the crazy shit that's happened since the last appointment. I have this one client who has six kids. I've never met them, and I don't remember their names. But let me tell you, I know so much about them. I call one the hippy kid, one the theater kid, one the kid having issues with high school snobs, and so on. I ask about each one. And if a client doesn't like someone or is mad at a friend, then I'm mad at them too. I can't help it; I'm invested. Sometimes with clients, I go through a divorce with them, or the death of a child or spouse. Sometimes I experience with them one of their children realizing they're gay. It's a beautiful thing. So no, I never get tired of this. This is where loyalty is born. You will be successful at this job if you just listen.

Honestly, the only time you can get "bored" is at the beginning of your career, especially being an assistant. You sort of stand around and watch a lot and maybe get to do a few blowouts and shampoos. But you control how bored you get; you can take that knowledge and practice. *Just go freaking practice.* Take this time to take it all in. When you're waiting for a walk-in, go watch a veteran stylist do a balayage or watch a balayage class on your phone. Make use of your free time and soak it all in. You'll also get bored waiting for your books to fill up. Don't just block off your schedule and get your nails done. Go and learn! I still find myself waiting for a client but watching the stylist across the way perform a service in a way I've never thought of doing.

If you get bored in cosmetology, you're the problem. You can find your spark anywhere—just pick another fork in the winding road of beauty and take another avenue. You have enormous options, always.

Me coloring a longtime client with my old assistant, Maddie Grabert, who now has a chair of her own.

10
FAKE IT TO MAKE IT

I feel like every stylist needs a tattoo of this saying: "Fake it to make it." That's the game. I remember the first time a client sat in my chair and asked for an "ombre." This was long ago, and no one in the entire salon had ever heard of it. In fact, I remember one of the stylists saying, "An Obama? What's that?" I told the client, "Absolutely!" The client then showed me a few pics, and I ran to the back and researched it on my phone. I even hurried up and watched a few quick tutorials. I faked that appointment so hard and literally had sweat marks on my clothes when she left. I must admit, it was pretty good, but definitely a building block for me to improve my ombre services.

That's what being a hairstylist really is. Learn the fundamentals in school, get out into the salon, get asked to do all types of services. Fake it like you absolutely know what you're doing, even though you have armpit sweat and do not feel very confident, and hope they'll rebook with you so you can perfect the service next time. It's all about faking it to make it. Fake that you know what you're doing, try your best not to screw it up, ask as many of the veteran stylists in the break room (or your teachers) to get a good game plan, use your fundamentals from school, and walk out there cool, calm, and collected and sure they feel comfortable with you. You *never* want to make them feel like they have a new stylist who doesn't know what they're doing. They smell that fear like bloodhounds. Also, talk them through the service and why you're doing certain things. It shows you are making educated decisions and you know what you're talking about. It also takes away that "surprise" ending I was talking about earlier. Don't do that. Walk them through the service. Tell them why you're blow-drying it this way or why you're curling it that way. They'll trust you more—next time you won't have to *fake* it as much.

You can ask almost every stylist out there, and I'm pretty sure they will agree with me: They learned everything they know now from being in a salon. In school, you just learn what will get you the license and a few other things. You will learn everything else from watching and experimenting in the salon. Hence the saying "Fake it to make it." You have no idea how many clients I performed "firsts" on, and they had no idea. I deserve an Oscar.

The last thing in this section—because it really gets under my skin—is to practice something outside the salon once you've had to ask for help on it. Please start practicing this in school before you get to a salon. Example: Say a client comes in and asks you to do something you've never done before or something you haven't had a lot of practice with yet. Let's pretend it's a pixie cut they're asking for. Then a teacher or a veteran stylist comes over and walks you through it or teaches you how to cut a pixie. Once that service has finished and the pixie client has left, *do not just wait for the next time that service walks in again* to be the next time you perform a pixie. I cannot stand that. Take what that teacher or stylist taught you and go home and practice that pixie on a mannequin or friend or something.

PRO TIP

Get business cards—you won't need a lot; most of everything is on social media. I even made some while I was in school. When your waiter brings your bill, slip a card in the receipt book. When you're at the checkout at a grocery store, spark up a convo about hair and give the cashier a card. Have them handy. Write 20 percent discount on it to make them feel special if you want. Get a badass, unique card.

Go watch a crapload of videos on it. You don't just watch the teacher or veteran stylist that one time and wait for the next client to come in months later and hope you do it better. That's laziness, and that's relying on someone else to do your work for you—not cool. I love when newer stylists ask me questions, but I hate when I continuously have to help them every time that same technique comes in. All that shows me is that the stylist did not "study" or practice or try to make themselves better at it. Don't be that person.

You will mess up. And that's OK. It's not the end of the world, and you will learn from it and hopefully never do it again. I'll never forget my first mess-up. A guy came in for his second visit and said, "The same as last time." I was still very new and wasn't aware of how important it was to truly remember every aspect of what you performed on a client. I politely said, "Um, what guard would you like to start with at the bottom near your neck?" He said a #2 to a #3, which means, start with a #2 guard near the neck and fade into a #3 guard near the top. But the way he used his hands when touching his head looked like he pointed to the top of his head when he confirmed #3. So what did I do? I used my clippers and shaved it with a #2 guard all around his head and started shaving the *top* of his head with a #3 guard, like a freaking buzz cut. His eyes when I shaved it right down the middle of his head with a #3 is a look I will *never* forget. He said, "What are you doing?"

I said, "Doing a number two to a number three, just like you said."

He said, "No, I meant a number two faded into a number three on the sides. I wear the top of my hair spiked up with some length."

I have never in my life been so red in the face. Trust me, I saw myself in the mirror at that moment. Just typing out this moment makes me want to vomit.

Here's the best part: After the shock was over and me apologizing way too much and probably aggravating him, we laughed about it. I then cut his hair and gained his beautiful wife and daughter as clients and cut all their hair for another decade. He's one of the coolest people on the planet, and he taught me one of the biggest lessons in my career—*remember what you do on every client.*

So fake it to make it. Be realistic; there is no stylist on this planet who knows absolutely everything about hair. Trends keep coming, and you must keep exploring them. When you don't know how to do something, look it up, ask a veteran, practice, take a class, whatever! But don't let your client see you sweat.

11
SHUT UP AND DO IT

I think I've pretty much covered all I can to at least give you a glimpse into this world of beauty. If you've gotten this far in the book, you must be getting a little serious about this. I'm proud of you. That's a big step. Buying and finishing this book makes you that much more prepared to make the jump than you were yesterday. This world is not for the weary. You will not just go to school, get out, get into your favorite salon, and take off with a crapload of money in your account without doing at least some of the things I've mentioned. Remember: "You're only as good as the training you do when no one is looking."

If you take this trade lightly, your bank account will reflect it. If you don't respect this industry, it won't respect you. If you don't view yourself as a professional, neither will your peers or your clients. Take pride in your brand and your work. If you don't, no one else will. You've read the book, so now cipher through this info. Go ahead—be a nerd and be proud of it. Write all in this book. Start that page on what schools are around you. Practice telling a friend you trust about your plans to go to cosmetology school. You've seriously got this—stop being a scaredy-cat.

All right, people, I'm done. I'm signing out. But listen to me: Just because you bought this book and read it doesn't mean you're done with me. Reach out and find me on social media: @melissagoudeauhair or @soyouwannabea-hairstylist and soyouwannabeahairstylist.com. If you have a question, ask me. Don't be shy. Just send me a message that you read the book. Show me a pic of your dog. I don't care. Just keep in touch. I'm pretty sure that's what I was put on this earth to do—help people. You've got this—I promise. And remember: if you don't "got this," fake it to make it. I'm cheering for you.

Love, peace, and hair grease,
Melissa Pittman Goudeau

PS: Be on the lookout for my next books.

Pretty sure I'd like to write a book on stylists and the dreaded taxes and how to do them and all that crap. Someone needs to put it into words that make sense to people who fix hair for a living and don't crunch numbers.

Pretty sure I'd like to write a book on becoming a better stylist once you're in the business. There's so much more I wanted to say in this book, but it just didn't make sense to put it in here for those just starting in the industry.

Pretty sure I'd like to write a book for stylists wanting to become salon owners. That is for real a whole other world that could probably take up a series. Just because you're great at hair doesn't mean you'd be great at running a business—think about that, please!

ACKNOWLEDGMENTS

For someone who has never written a book before, I kept this secret (of me writing this book) for years. As I came across certain individuals who I trusted and knew they would encourage me and cheer me on, I sparingly told a few, especially special people who I knew could help me with their wisdom or talent. Here are a few . . . .

Mark Palermo, (the newly retired) CEO of the Vanguard Nation and Vanguard Paul Mitchell Systems. When you work with the Paul Mitchell community, the entire family is our cheerleaders. I contacted him and told him about my book adventure, and he treated me to lunch. We spent almost two hours talking about how he could help me. He's truly an inspirational leader, and I was extremely fortunate to have a successful entrepreneur such as himself giving me advice on this endeavor.

Cami Ezernack, my secret keeper. Her encouragement and talent carried me through those last months of writing this book. She did my makeup for the cover—she's a wizard—and read my book first to see if I left anything out.

Alysson Foti Bourque, a friend from high school who happens to be an award-winning author of children's books *The Alycat Series*. She was the only author I personally knew and could trust to take me along this book journey.

She pointed me in the directions I needed to go, kept my secret, and read all of my emails about publishing that I needed to have translated. Thank you, Alysson, for your guidance, wisdom, friendship, and trustworthiness.

Catherine Goudeau Brignac, my business partner, friend, and sister-in-law. It's nice to own a salon with someone who not only pulls their weight but excels in it. She's amazing at her job as co-owner and even took this book home and scribbled some notes in it that she thought I should add. She's my work wife, and I wouldn't want to share this job with anyone else. She's a kick-ass hairstylist, and I love watching her work magic every day.

Lindsey Romero—throughout the book, you'll notice the amazing photography that is from Lindsey, one of my former English students. I called her up, trusted her to keep my secret, and she said she was all in. She's truly talented and has become a master of her craft. You definitely need to check out her work. She's amazing with business photography as well. Go follow her on IG @LindseyRomeroMedia. She's a baddie in the photography world.

I'd love to thank **McKenzie Turley, Stephanie Kocielski, and Larissa Love** for their wisdom and sidebar talk you found on some pages. These big celebrity hairstylists took a chance on little ol' me and trusted my vision. I hope if I ever get up to their level of success I can return the favor to another stylist.

To my first readers—Cami Ezernack, Catherine Brignac, Regina Pittman, Clint Pittman, Lindsey Romero, Phyllis Bel, Joy Blanchard, Alysson Foti Bourque, and David Goudeau.

BIBLIOGRAPHY

"Barbers, Hairstylists, and Cosmetologists." US Bureau of Labor Statistics. September 13, 2002. http:// bls.gov/ooh/personal-care-and-service/Barbers-hairstylists-and-cosmetologists.htm.

Claybaugh, Brennan, Winn Claybaugh, Elecia Elrod-Howard, Gail Fink, Eric Manuel, Keri Manuel, Barb Toberman, Shawn Claybough. *Business Fundamentals: Connecting to My Future*. Louisiana: Vanguard Publishing, 2018.

"Hair Stylists, Demographics and Statistics in the US." Zippia. September 9, 2022. http://zippia.com/hair-stylists-jobs/demographics/.

ABOUT THE AUTHOR

Melissa Pittman Goudeau, a resident of Youngsville, Louisiana, is a co-owner of the Cut House Salon, an amazing twenty-stylist salon in Lafayette, Louisiana. Melissa graduated as a Ragin' Cajun from the University of Louisiana at Lafayette. She graduated in secondary English and became an honors English teacher at a Lafayette high school. After teaching for a while, she finally mustered up the courage to begin her longtime dream of completing cosmetology school. After three years as a stylist, she opened the Cut House Salon with a partner. While at her salon, Melissa has become a master at Invisible Bead Extensions and has built a full clientele. After being asked for advice on going to cosmetology school from many clients—asking for themselves, a friend, or their child—Melissa searched for resources to refer to about the beauty industry. When she realized the absence of these resources, she began writing *So You Wanna Be a Hairstylist.* She hopes this book will help aid those who are thinking about a career in beauty.